"Kyle Idleman is never boring. He never lulls. Just the opposite. Kyle always stirs, excites, and challenges. By the end of this book you will see grace in a new light; you will see your loving God in a new light. Read it and be encouraged."

Max Lucado, author of *GRACE* and *In the Grip of Grace*

"Grace is my favorite topic, and Kyle Idleman's new book breathes fresh life into it through engaging stories and winsome insights. Nothing is greater than grace. Celebrate it, live it, share it!"

Lee Strobel, award-winning author of *The Case for Grace*

"Kyle Idleman is a remarkable writer. As he opens his heart and God's Word, he shares stories that are both moving and meaningful and confesses his own weaknesses with stunning transparency. He also has a wry sense of humor, which enhances and never detracts from the important lessons he offers. *Grace Is Greater* is practical and inspirational, providing a clear path to freedom through God's amazing gift of grace. I loved it!"

Liz Curtis Higgs, bestselling author of *Bad Girls of the Bible*

"As a follower of Jesus, I can't help but being a fan of Kyle Idleman. He seems to eat, sleep, and breathe a passion for heart-connection with God. That kind of a relationship can't happen when we confine God's grace to the work he did to save us. It happens when we allow his grace to permeate the messiest parts of our lives and ultimately become the defining feature of how we treat others. Kyle's book *Grace Is Greater* is a journey in how to make that happen."

Dr. Tim Kimmel, author of *Grace Based Parenting* and *Grace Filled Marriage*

"Kyle Idleman's books never cease to inspire me. He writes with boldness, communicating biblical truth in a fresh and convicting way! Kyle challenges us to not just experience grace but to make sure no one we come in contact with misses the grace of God. His witty, straightforward wisdom will motivate and encourage you to live a life worthy of your calling. I highly recommend it!"

Chip Ingram, author of *Grace: Experiencing God's Generosity*

"If Kyle Idleman writes something, I read it! I sat down to read *Grace Is Greater* and couldn't put it down. His teaching on grace challenged me. The way God is presented comforted me. The words that describe people inspired me! I'm different and better because of this book . . . and you will be too."

Caleb Kaltenbach, author of *Messy Grace*

"When I was sent the manuscript for *Grace Is Greater*, I thought, *Oh no, not another book on grace!* I quickly checked my little library and discovered that I already had at least eight books whose titles included the word *grace*. I asked myself, *Do I need another one?* But I began to read and was immediately drawn in by Kyle Idleman's engaging stories, delightful humor, compelling truths, and, yes, grace. I laughed out loud and shed a few tears as I was reminded in fresh ways of the all-encompassing greatness, power, and relevance of God's grace for the brokenness, disappointments, and hurts we all encounter on our journey. After reading *Grace Is Greater*, I decided the answer to my question was, *Yes, I do need another book on grace*. I think we all do."

Cynthia Heald, author of *Becoming a Woman of Grace*

"Kyle has a way of communicating grace that invites all people to partake. In *Grace Is Greater*, you will be challenged to receive

God's love and mercy daily, and freely give it to others. From the first page to the last, you will see that grace is truly greater than anything and everything else."

Mark Batterson, lover of God's grace and *New York Times* bestselling author of *The Circle Maker*

"Kyle cuts through all the nonsense and takes us straight to what is most important spiritually."

Jud Wilhite, author of *Uncensored Grace*

"Unlike the quacks-like-a-duck test, just because a book talks about grace doesn't mean it knows grace. Fortunately for us, Kyle Idleman's *Grace Is Greater* both talks and knows grace. Read this for yourself. Then share it with someone, no strings attached, just like grace."

John D. Blase, poet and author of *All Is Grace* (with Brennan Manning)

"*Grace Is Greater* is a beautiful narrative encapsulating not just the beauty and sanctity of God's grace, but the way his grace finds us and meets us at the foot of the mountains we all face, the way it pulls us up, cleanses us so thoroughly, and invites us into the incredible arms of forgiveness. *Grace Is Greater* is an invitation to delve into your own spirit; let go of the worries, regrets, and assumptions that are holding you captive; and fully receive God's love on its most basic and wildly profound levels."

Emily Ley, author of *Grace, Not Perfection*

"Kyle has a way with words; when his pen touches paper, God uses him to stir our soul and expand our imagination. In *Grace Is Greater*, you will learn that God's grace is greater than your mistakes, your hurts, and your circumstances. You are going to love this book."

Derwin Gray, author of *Crazy Grace for Crazy Times*

"If you're tired of running away from your mistakes, your hurts, and your circumstances, read this book. With spot-on biblical truth, riveting stories, and poignant applications, Kyle Idleman will lead you to the grace place. As you personally apply the truths in *Grace Is Greater*, you'll find yourself chased by grace and embraced by God. Buy one copy for yourself and ten more to give away!"

Carol Kent, author of *Between a Rock and a Grace Place*

GRACE
IS GREATER

God's Plan to Overcome Your Past, Redeem Your Pain,
and Rewrite Your Story

kyle idleman

BakerBooks
a division of Baker Publishing Group
Grand Rapids, Michigan

Published by Baker Books
a division of Baker Publishing Group
P.O. Box 6287, Grand Rapids, MI 49516-6287
www.bakerbooks.com

Printed in the United States of America

Library of Congress Cataloging-in-Publication Data
Names: Idleman, Kyle, author.
Title: Grace is greater : God's plan to overcome your past, redeem your pain, and rewrite your story / Kyle Idleman.
Description: Grand Rapids, MI : Baker Books, a division of Baker Publishing Group, [2017] | Includes bibliographical references.
Identifiers: LCCN 2016041079 | ISBN 9780801019418 (pbk.)
Subjects: LCSH: Grace (Theology)
Classification: LCC BT761.3 .I55 2017 | DDC 234—dc23
LC record available at https://lccn.loc.gov/2016041079

Published in association with Don Gates of the literary agency The Gates Group, www.the-gates-group.com.

Some names and details have been changed to protect the privacy of the individuals involved.

In keeping with biblical principles of creation stewardship, Baker Publishing Group advocates the responsible use of our natural resources. As a member of the Green Press Initiative, our company uses recycled paper when possible. The text paper of this book is composed in part of post-consumer waste.

17   18   19   20   21   22   23   7   6   5   4   3   2   1

CONTENTS

Prologue   9

Introduction: Grace Is Greater   13

Part 1: Grace Is Greater . . . Than Your Mistakes

1. More Forgiving Than Your Guilt   21

2. More Beautiful Than Your Brokenness   33

3. More Redemptive Than Your Regrets   49

Part 2: Grace Is Greater . . . Than Your Hurts

4. More Healing Than Your Wounds   65

5. More Freeing Than Your Bitterness   87

6. More Prevailing Than Your Vengeance   103

7. More Reconciling Than Your Resentment   117

Part 3: Grace Is Greater . . . Than Your Circumstances

8. More Peaceful Than Your Disappointments   133

9. More Powerful Than Your Weakness   151

10. More Hopeful Than Your Despair   169

Notes   187

PROLOGUE

Five years ago I was traveling around the country speaking at different churches and conferences on the subject of following Jesus. I had written a book called *Not a Fan* that challenged those who called themselves Christians to not be fans of Jesus but followers of Jesus. When Jesus invited us to follow him, he was inviting us to deny ourselves and take up a cross. Our tendency, especially in the Western world, is to try to follow Jesus without having to deny ourselves. We want to accept the invitation of Jesus but we are obsessed with being comfortable, which means we try to follow Jesus without carrying a cross.

In other words, we want to follow Jesus close enough to get the benefits but not so close that it requires anything from us. When Jesus offered his invitation, he made people uncomfortable. So uncomfortable, in fact, that it wasn't unusual for large crowds to turn around and go home.

As I preached this message, I usually would get pretty worked up. I wanted Christians to feel convicted and uncomfortable with the idea that it was fine to follow Jesus on their terms rather than his. One night I was in Birmingham, Alabama, preaching at a men's conference at the University of Alabama. I tend to get especially hard-core when I'm talking to a room filled with thousands of men. After I finished my talk, I walked offstage feeling pretty good about beating up thousands of men at the same time. I stayed for a while afterward and greeted some of the men and signed some books. One of them handed me a piece of paper with a Scripture reference scribbled on it.

Hebrews 12:15

I didn't ask him what it said. I know this sounds a bit pathetic, but if someone brings up a Scripture reference I'm most likely going to act as if I know what it says even if I have no idea. You could totally be making it up and I'll probably still nod my head as if I'm not only familiar with that reference but committed it to memory when I was but a lad. Anyway, I thanked him and jammed the piece of paper into my pocket and forgot about it.

One of two things happens to most anything that has the misfortune of finding itself in my pocket. It either ends up in the trash in a wad of broken toothpicks and gum wrappers or more likely just stays in my jeans pocket until it goes through enough cycles of laundry that it eventually dissolves into lint that ends up on the collecting screen in the dryer.

But as I was heading home that night I stopped at a drive-through for a late-night snack. When I checked my pocket for change I pulled out that piece of paper. While I was waiting on my food I pulled Hebrews 12:15 up on my phone. I was familiar with the verse, but when I read it this time it was different. Have you ever encountered a verse of Scripture where it feels less like you reading it and more like God is reading it to you? It was like that.

See to it that no one misses the grace of God.*

Since that night at the drive-through God has taken me on a journey toward writing this book. I still like to challenge people with what it means to follow Jesus completely, but in the back of my mind I'm constantly hearing the Holy Spirit whisper to me, *See to it that no one misses the grace of God.*

The word translated "misses" could also be translated "fails to receive" or "fails to obtain" or "fails to experience." My prayer for you as you read this book is that you would receive, obtain, and experience the grace of God in your life.

*Hebrews 12:15 NIV 1984.

INTRODUCTION

Grace Is Greater

At the beginning of every year you can find an article or two that updates readers on new words that have been added to the dictionary. I always find it fascinating to see a word that didn't exist, or at least wasn't officially recognized a year ago, break into our official vocabulary.

Mind you, I don't often use these new words because purposely using words people aren't familiar with seems somewhat puerile, maybe even a bit jejune. But this year as I read these newly recognized words, I decided to entertain myself by trying to guess the meaning of the word before I read its definition. It was more challenging than I anticipated. Let me give you three of my favorite new words, and you try to guess their meaning:

phonesia
disconfect
blamestorming

Got your own definitions? Here come the real ones.

1. *Phonesia.* I thought this word was most likely a noun some-how related to "phone" and "amnesia." Here was my guess at a definition: "The phenomenon of forgetting where you left your cell phone a few moments after using it." Here's the real definition: "The act of dialing a phone number and forgetting who you were calling just as the person answers."

2. *Disconfect.* I'll give you a hint: this word may be helpful to use around Halloween time. Here's an example of the word being used in a sentence: "The boy asked his mother if he could eat the piece of candy since he had disconfected it." Here's the definition: "The attempt to sterilize a piece of candy that has been dropped on the ground by blowing on it."

3. *Blamestorming.* This word might be useful in a corporate setting. Clearly it's a play on the word *brainstorming.* Here's the definition: "Sitting in a group and discussing who's responsible for the company's problems rather than trying to solve them."

Those are some new words with new meanings. They are interesting and capture our attention for this reason: they are new and yet they define something familiar.

Grace is not a new word to us. It's familiar—and that can be a problem. When you're using a word that has been around a long time and has been talked about frequently, people tend to yawn. The word *grace* is so common it doesn't feel very amazing.

I remember a Kellogg's Corn Flakes commercial that came out when I was a kid. Apparently the people at Kellogg's did some research and found out that a lot of their potential consumers had grown up eating Kellogg's Corn Flakes but had not purchased a box in recent years. So they came up with a campaign slogan that went like this: "Kellogg's Corn Flakes—Taste them again for the first time." They wanted to reintroduce people to their product, so they invited them to try Kellogg's Corn Flakes as if they never had before.

I know that many of you have heard countless sermons about grace. You may have even read a number of books about grace. But my prayer is that you would see this word again for the first time.

Root of Bitterness

Hebrews 12:15 says, "See to it that no one misses the grace of God" (NIV 1984). This command is followed by a warning of what happens when someone does miss it:

> And that no bitter root grows up to cause trouble and defile many. (v. 15 NIV 1984)

When we miss grace, a bitter root begins to grow. In Hebrew culture any poisonous plant would be called a "bitter" plant. The author of Hebrews uses "bitter root" as a metaphor to make it clear that when we miss grace things become toxic. Religion without grace is poisonous. A relationship without grace is poisonous. A church without grace is poisonous. A heart without grace is poisonous. The bitter root may be small and slow in its growth, but eventually the poison takes effect.

When we miss grace, things become toxic.

In this book we will be looking at the greatness of grace and the effect it has on our lives, but let's be clear: there is also a non-grace effect. When we miss grace, the poison of bitterness and anger will eventually become too much to keep buried. The poison of guilt and shame will eventually destroy a soul.

Experiencing Grace

Numerous theological books teach the doctrine of grace, and some of them have helped me enormously. To be clear, though, this is not one of those. You're still welcome to write a blog post or send me an email pointing this out, but it won't be much fun because I'll be quick to agree with you. I'm less interested, and for that matter less qualified, to teach you about the doctrine of grace. I am much more interested in helping you *experience* grace. I tend to think grace is best and most fully understood not by way of explanation alone but through experience.

Think of it like romantic love. If you want to understand romantic love, you can open a scientific textbook and have romantic love explained in terms of neural and chemical reactions. And that might be helpful, but there's really only one way to understand romantic love. It must be experienced.

And when something is best understood through experience, it's best taught through stories. Stories bring you into an experience. The Bible is full of narratives that teach us about grace. When Jesus wanted to help people understand the grace of God, he didn't give a lengthy and detailed explanation. Instead he told the story of the prodigal son.

Compare what we learn about grace from Paul with what we learn about grace from Jesus. Paul uses the word *grace* more than a hundred times in his letters as he helps the church understand grace. Jesus, on the other hand, never used the word *grace*. Instead he showed us what it looked like. Both approaches are helpful and needed, and certainly Paul's explanations were motivated by his own experience of grace and his desire for others to experience it. But if grace is explained without being experienced, it really doesn't have much effect. To repurpose E. B. White's famous quip about humor, "Grace can be dissected like a frog, but the thing dies in the process."

I've sat through several seminary classes taking detailed notes on the subject of grace. I've memorized countless Bible verses that describe grace. I've read numerous books about grace. But do you know what has taught me the most about grace? My own story and the stories of others who have experienced grace.

God's grace is compelling when explained but irresistible when experienced.

God's grace is compelling when explained but irresistible when experienced.

It's my prayer that you won't miss grace but rather will powerfully experience the grace effect in your life—and no matter what you have done, no matter what has been done to you, you will personally experience the truth that grace is *greater*.

Grace is powerful enough to erase your guilt.

Grace is big enough to cover your shame.

Grace is real enough to heal your relationships.

Grace is strong enough to hold you up when you're weak.

Grace is sweet enough to cure your bitterness.

Grace is satisfying enough to deal with your disappointment.

Grace is beautiful enough to redeem your brokenness.

Grace explained is necessary, but grace experienced is essential.

PART 1

Grace Is Greater . . .
Than Your Mistakes

More Forgiving Than Your Guilt

My son has always taken Halloween trick-or-treating very seriously.* He literally maps out the neighborhood, carefully routing his course so he doesn't miss a single house. This is not about having fun collecting candy. This is a competition to be won, a mission to complete. He chooses his costumes for mobility purposes. At the end of each competition, he brings his bag of candy in and weighs it. Then he organizes it. He gets that impulse from his momma. He separates all the chocolates and freezes them. He organizes the rest by kind and color.

I knew all that. What I *didn't* know is that he also creates a spreadsheet to track how many pieces of candy he has collected, how many he has eaten, and how many he has left.

When he was nine years old, his bag weighed in at 5.8 pounds. He went to bed that Halloween night and I did what I normally

*If you're already upset because I let my son trick-or-treat, please remember that you're reading about grace.

do—stole a young child's treasure while he slept. I decided he'd never notice if a few pieces of Laffy Taffy went missing, so I took three pieces and destroyed the evidence. The next day I came home from work, opened the front door, and found he was waiting for me. He said, "Dad, we need to talk." He sat me down and asked, "Is there anything you'd like to tell me?" I was now feeling a little nervous and wondered if my wife sold me out.* Then he pulled out a piece of paper with numbers and symbols I couldn't decode, looked me in the eye, and told me he knew I'd eaten three pieces of taffy.

I never thought I'd get caught, but it turns out he was keeping track of his candy. I would have denied it to my son, but his evidence was strong and this was not my first offense. Instead of telling him I was sorry, I took the opportunity to point out some details to my son that he may have overlooked. For example, that I made his existence possible.

Obviously a few pieces of candy aren't that big of a deal, but here's what I discovered about myself in that moment: when I'm guilty of something, even if it's not a big deal, I have a tendency to be defensive. I do not like to admit guilt. I will passionately defend myself, irrationally justify myself, and almost always minimize the seriousness of what I've done.

If that's how I respond to being accused of stealing three pieces of Laffy Taffy, chances are I'm not going to respond with much honesty or humility when it comes to the sin in my life. Everything in me wants to deny, compare, minimize, and justify. But as long as I approach my sin with that kind of spirit, I won't be able to experience the power and greatness of God's grace.

*He probably paid her off with Junior Mints.

The Ugly Truth

Our ability to appreciate grace is in direct correlation to the degree to which we acknowledge our need for it. The more I recognize the ugliness of my sin, the more I can appreciate the beauty of God's grace. The Bible holds up a mirror and confronts us with the reality of our sin.

> Everyone has sinned; we all fall short of God's glorious standard. (Rom. 3:23 NLT)

So who does "everyone" include? Well, everyone includes you and everyone includes me. We have all sinned. I'm sure you've heard that before. I doubt it's new information. My question is, how do you respond to that information? For a long time I would read verses like that and think to myself, *Well, yeah. I mean, technically, I've sinned. But I haven't* sin *sinned.*

The more I recognize the ugliness of my sin, the more I can appreciate the beauty of God's grace.

Here's the way it usually gets worded to me: "I'm not *that* bad."

My wife and I were eating dinner together at a restaurant when a woman, probably in her late fifties, came over and introduced herself. She began to tell her story of how she had recently become a Christian. Except she didn't say "Christian," she said "follower of Jesus." She pointed out her husband seated at a table across the restaurant. I think she felt like she needed to address why he didn't come with her to say hello. She explained he wasn't upset about her decision but seemed annoyed by it and didn't understand. I smiled and waved at him. He waved but didn't smile. His wave was like the wave you give the other driver at a four-way stop when you tell them to go ahead even though you think you have the right-of-way. That kind of wave. I went over and introduced myself, and we chatted for a minute or two.

The next day I followed up with an email to both of them saying it was good to meet them and to let me know if either of them had any questions I could help with. I didn't hear anything back for a couple of months. And then one day I was sitting at my desk when I got an email from the husband. He told me about the changes he had seen in his wife. She was kinder and more patient. She seemed more joyful. But instead of being excited about these changes, he was skeptical. Here's a line from his email: "She seems much happier now, but I think she's just trying to get me to drink the Kool Aid."

I knew that this wasn't a rhetorical email. He was reaching out but didn't want to say it. I emailed him back and asked if he would come to church with his wife and visit with me for a few minutes after a service.

We sat in a small room, and I began to tell him the Good News of the gospel. I began with Romans 3:23 and made the point that everyone has sinned and fallen short of God's standard. Immediately he became defensive and said, "I'm not that bad. Most people would consider me a good man." He thought it unfair to be called a sinner and be judged by "God's standard."

"How fair is it to set a standard that no one can meet and then say everyone is a sinner?" he continued. "It's like setting up a target that's out of range and then blaming the shooter for not being able to hit it."

I started my attempt at a theological explanation of why we were sinners. I was going to begin with Adam and Eve in the Garden of Eden and talk about how sin entered the world. I think he would have been impressed with some of the terms I was going to use to explain how we have rebelled against God. But before I had a chance to talk about imputation or ancestral sin, his wife interrupted me and asked if she could say something.

She didn't wait for my permission. She turned toward her husband and said, "Do you think it's OK to get drunk and yell at your spouse? Do you think it's OK to lie about your sales numbers? Do you think it's OK to tell your grandson you'll be at his game and then not show up?" And she asked three or four more personal questions that were clearly indicting. His answers to these questions were obvious. Then she said, "You say it's not fair to be held to God's standard, but you fall short of your own standards."

> As long as we think I'm not that bad, grace will never seem that good.

I had never thought of it that way. We may get defensive when a preacher calls us a sinner—but forget about God's standard, we can't even meet our own standard.

We work hard at convincing ourselves and others we're not that bad, but the truth is we are worse than we ever imagined. The more you push back on that, the more you push back on experiencing God's grace. If we miss the reality and the depth of our sin, we miss out on the grace of God.

As long as we think *I'm not that bad*, grace will never seem that good. We usually come to the conclusion that we are not that bad a couple of different ways.

1. We compare ourselves to others.

It's not that we claim to be perfect, but when we compare ourselves with others, what we have done doesn't seem to be that big of a deal. And of course, when we are judging ourselves we usually give ourselves a big break. Compared to what a lot of people are doing, our sins amount to little more than jaywalking or loitering.

We dismiss our sin and our need for grace by comparing ourselves to others, but do you know what you're doing when you compare yourself to other people and feel superior to them? Yep, you're sinning. And it's likely that from where God sits, your pride and self-righteousness are uglier than the sins of the person you just compared yourself to.

2. We weigh the bad against the good.

Last year I read a *New York Times* interview with New York City's former mayor Michael Bloomberg. At the time Bloomberg was seventy-two years old. He was being interviewed just before his fiftieth college reunion. Bloomberg talked about how sobering it was to realize how many of his classmates had passed away. But the journalist, Jeremy Peters, observed that Bloomberg didn't seem too worried about what waited for him on the other side. Peters wrote:

> But if [Bloomberg] senses that he may not have as much time left as he would like, he has little doubt about what would await him at a Judgment Day. Pointing to his work on gun safety, obesity and smoking cessation, he said with a grin: "I am telling you if there is a God, when I get to heaven I'm not stopping to be interviewed. I am heading straight in. I have earned my place in heaven. It's not even close."[1]

From his perspective grace isn't needed or wanted. He puts the good he has done on one side of the scale and decides he's not going to need any help.

We can all find ways to reach the conclusion that *I'm not that bad*, but in doing so we miss out on God's great gift of grace. Until we recognize our need for grace, we won't care about receiving it.

Our default is to cover up our sin or at the very least minimize it. But in covering up our sin we are covering up grace. In minimizing sin we are diminishing the joy that comes with forgiveness. Jesus didn't try to make people feel better about themselves by diminishing the seriousness of their sin and falsely reassuring them that they were not that bad. Jesus explained that the one who is forgiven much loves much (see Luke 7:47). He paralleled our love for God with the degree of forgiveness we have received.

The Biggest Sinner I Know

I read a quote on Twitter the other day from a pastor named Jean Larroux. I inwardly protested as soon as I read it, but ironically my protest likely only did more to prove the truth of what he said. Here's the quote: "If the biggest sinner you know isn't you, then you don't know yourself very well."

My immediate and instinctual response to that quote was, *Well, look, I'm a sinner. In fact, I'm a big sinner. But I'm not the* biggest *sinner I know.* But the more I think about that quote, and the more I'm honest with myself and my motives, the more difficulty I have denying it.

There was something about that quote that seemed familiar to me. I couldn't quite put my finger on it until I was rereading the familiar passage of Scripture where Paul identifies himself to Timothy as the chief of sinners:

> Here is a trustworthy saying that deserves full acceptance: Christ Jesus came into the world to save sinners—of whom I am the worst. (1 Tim. 1:15)

I remembered writing a paper about this passage when I was in seminary. My paper focused on Paul's past before he became a Christian. I made the case that Paul describes himself as the worst of sinners because he had been a persecutor of Christians and did everything he could to destroy the church and the cause of Christ. When my professor returned the paper to me, there was no grade at the top of the page. Instead, in red ink, he had written "Rewrite."

I wasn't sure what the problem was. He hadn't made any notes in the margin to help me understand why I needed to start over on the entire paper. After class I went up to his desk, hoping to get a little feedback. Then he took out his red pen and he circled one word from 1 Timothy 1:15.

> Here is a trustworthy saying that deserves full acceptance: Christ Jesus came into the world to save sinners—of whom I **am** the worst.

I waited for a moment, expecting him to expound, but he had already moved on to the next student. I stood there staring at that one word *am*. Suddenly I realized what I had missed. The verb *am* is present tense. And that changed everything. Paul didn't say, "I *was* the worst of sinners." He said, "I *am* the worst of sinners."

If you were to hook me up to a lie detector test and ask me, "Do you think you're the worst sinner?" I would probably say yes because I'm so sinful that I'll try to make myself seem more spiritual by sounding as humble as possible.* But I'm fairly certain the polygraph machine would reveal the truth. If I'm honest, deep down, probably not even that deep, I don't consider myself the worst of sinners. But I can tell you, the more I learn about the righteousness of God and the more I examine my own life and motives—the closer I'm getting to the inescapable conclusion that I am the worst sinner I know.

The Sickness of Sin

Romans 3:23 says that everyone has sinned. Romans 6:23 says the penalty for our sin is death. We can minimize what we have done, but the Bible says we have been declared guilty and sentenced to death.

As I am writing this chapter, I have been quarantined to the guest room. I have supposedly been sick for the last few days, and I'm supposed to be resting and getting better. On the nightstand next to me is some medicine my wife brought in to me a few hours ago. But she knows I won't take it. See, despite evidence to the contrary, I'm not convinced I'm actually sick. My wife would tell you I have a problem admitting when I'm not feeling well. For as long as possible I will refuse to concede that I'm sick. . . . Hold on a sec, she's coming in to check on me.

OK, I'm back.

Here's what just happened. She came in and told me to take the medicine she had brought earlier. I asked her, "Why would

*Don't judge; you're the one going around hooking people up to lie detector tests.

I take medicine if I'm not sick?" She walked over and put her hand on my forehead and said, "You feel a little warm to me. I think you have a fever." I felt my own forehead and assured her I was fine. She suggested I let her take my temperature. So I cracked a joke about how it wouldn't be accurate, because when she walks in the room my temperature goes up several degrees. She rolled her eyes, and as she left the room she said, "Well, just remember I'm not going to be kissing you until you get better."

I took the medicine.

I refuse to acknowledge I'm sick, because if I'm sick it means I have to do some things differently. If I admit to myself I'm sick, I have to take medicine and lie in bed, and I don't like taking medicine and staying in bed. And so my strategy is to deny the reality of my condition as long as possible. But it turns out pretending I'm not sick is not a very effective way to get better. The sooner I admit my illness, the sooner I will take medicine and start feeling better. The sooner I start feeling better, the sooner I will be kissing my wife. But the longer I refuse to acknowledge my sickness and the longer I refuse to take the medicine, the longer I put off feeling better.

Around 1,600 years ago, Augustine wrote in his *Confessions*, "My sin was all the more incurable because I did not think myself a sinner."[2] Until we come face-to-face with our terminal diagnosis, we will refuse the cure.

The Bible gives us our diagnosis—we all have a sickness called *sin*. It's a virus that has infected the whole world. Romans 5:12 explains it this way:

> When Adam sinned, sin entered the world. Adam's sin brought death, so death spread to everyone, for everyone sinned. (NLT)

We've all been diagnosed with sin and our condition is terminal—*the wages of sin is death*. But then Paul introduces us to an antidote called *grace*.

> For the sin of this one man, Adam, brought death to many. But even greater is God's wonderful grace and his gift of forgiveness to many through this other man, Jesus Christ. And the result of God's gracious gift is very different from the result of that one man's sin. For Adam's sin led to condemnation, but God's free gift leads to our being made right with God. . . . For the sin of this one man, Adam, caused death to rule over many. But even greater is God's wonderful grace and his gift of righteousness, for all who receive it will live in triumph over sin and death through this one man, Jesus Christ.
>
> Yes, Adam's one sin brings condemnation for everyone, but Christ's one act of righteousness brings a right relationship with God and new life for everyone. (vv. 15–18 NLT)

Paul sets up an equation. On one side of the equation is your sin, and your sin is worse than you can imagine. You can minimize it, rationalize it, and try to dismiss it, but you are terminally ill. On the other side of the equation is God's grace. When Jesus died on the cross his blood wasn't infected by sin, and he became the antidote that cures us. After putting your sin on one side and God's grace on the other, Paul solves the equation.

Grace is always greater—no matter what.

> Even greater is God's wonderful grace. (v. 15 NLT)

I can tell you confidently that you've done nothing so horrible that grace can't cover it. Grace is always greater—no matter what.

Making It Personal

One weekend in church I gave everyone a piece of paper with this equation:

$$\text{Grace} > \underline{\hspace{3cm}}$$

And I asked them to fill in the blank with their worst sin.

I'd like to ask you to take a turn at this. The only way for grace to be experienced is for you to personalize your need for it. Take a minute and fill in the blank of the equation below, and after you fill in the blank go ahead and solve the equation by circling either the "greater than" or "less than" sign.

$$\text{Grace} >/< \underline{\hspace{3cm}}$$

Paul's explanation in Romans 5 about the greatness of God's grace is really helpful. But an explanation of grace without experiencing grace is like being terminally ill and a doctor gives you lifesaving medicine but you refuse to take it.

The greatness of God's grace means I don't have to keep trying to convince myself I am "not that bad."

The truth is I am worse than I ever wanted to admit, but God's grace is greater than I ever could have imagined.

More Beautiful Than Your Brokenness

In 2009, I received the following message on Facebook from a man named Wes who was in his early forties.

> I don't know if you have any good "Facebook stories" but I think you might after you read this. I'm not exactly sure why, but I feel compelled by God to tell you this story. It goes all over the place . . . so bear with me.
>
> I have known I was adopted all my life. I was raised in a Christian home by two terrific people who could not have children of their own. I'm now happily married and have my own children whom I dearly love.
>
> I never had a desire to seek out my birth parents until a few years ago. I was attending a Christian retreat and one of the speakers was an older man who told about getting his girlfriend pregnant

and then secretly giving the child up for adoption. He explained that he had lived with constant guilt that eventually caused him to develop a hard heart and bitterness toward God. One day his daughter contacted him and told him that she forgave him and God did too. It changed this man's life and he spoke of the freedom and the healing he had found.

That story made me think of my own situation. I wondered if it would help my birth parents to know that I was doing OK. I was able to find the name of my birth father and contacted him. It became clear to me that I was right about the guilt and pain that could follow a person after making such a difficult decision. He had never told anyone about my birth. It seemed that it was probably best that I not interfere with his life or complicate things for him.

But then something happened. . . . One night I was lying in bed with my wife and one of your shows came on. I was already half asleep, but my wife was watching it. Suddenly, I was startled when my wife exclaimed, "Oh, my God! That's your cousin!" She was talking about you. She knew a lot more about my birth family than I did because she is the one who did all the research. I didn't believe her but after a little Google search I realized she was correct.

I hope you are not too shocked, but your uncle, David Idleman, is my birth father. I picked you to contact first because as [you are] a pastor I thought you might be used to giving counsel on difficult situations. I know that I also have a sister, but I don't know if she knows about me. I don't want to stir the family pot and create problems or difficult situations, but like I said, I felt like God compelled me to reach out.

When I read that Facebook message, immediately a lot of things made sense to me. I had grown up close to my uncle

Dave. He taught me how to slalom water-ski when I was a kid and gave me a few karate lessons when I was in middle school. But as I grew older, I could tell my uncle carried a heavy weight wherever he went. Keeping a secret like that for so many years wearies a man. His eyes often seemed tired to me, worn out, like he was always just getting off a long day at work.

My uncle Dave somehow missed grace when his girlfriend became pregnant. He shouldn't have missed it. He grew up in a church environment and his girlfriend's father was a pastor. He shouldn't have missed grace, but somehow it didn't get communicated. Carrying around the guilt and shame of a secret for decades takes a toll on a man's heart.

When the secret about my uncle Dave's son came out, it was overwhelming for him. For decades he had lived with the weight of it and the fear of people finding out. What would my dad, his older brother, say? How would his parents, my grandparents, respond? Would they feel cheated out of knowing their grandchild? And what about his daughter, my cousin? She had grown up as an only child. She had always wanted a brother. But he never told her. He never told anyone.

And what about Wes? My uncle Dave had to think that his son would be angry at him. He could have felt abandoned and rejected his entire life. But now there was no hiding.

Sometimes our sin stays hidden because we are in denial or because our pride has blinded us to it. But oftentimes we try to keep our sin a secret because we just can't deal with what we've done. So we do our best not to think about the mistakes we've made or the sins we've committed, and we try to steer clear of God. How could he possibly forgive us when we can't even forgive ourselves?

Before Adam and Eve sinned in the Garden of Eden, the Bible says they lived life *naked and unashamed*. But the moment sin came on the scene, they were ashamed and did their best to hide from God.

Sometimes when our secret sin gets exposed and we can no longer hide it, then *we* go into hiding. As much as possible, we do our best to avoid the people who know. Shame becomes our constant companion who relentlessly whispers, *You're not worthy of forgiveness. You don't deserve a second chance.*

> You can run away and hide, but grace is relentless. Grace will chase you down.

But here's a surprising characteristic about grace—*grace chases you*. You can run away and hide, but grace is relentless. Grace will chase you down. That's what's happening to some of you right now, and you don't even know it. With every word you read, grace is gaining ground.

As a pastor, I love witnessing the moment grace finally catches up to someone's mess. The phrase I use to describe that moment is "beautiful collision." Those two words don't seem to go together. *Collision* brings to mind words like *broken, busted,* and *wrecked*—not typically words that fit with beautiful. But the Gospels are full of beautiful collisions. When a broken, busted, and wrecked life collides with Jesus, it's a beautiful thing.

Crash Course with Grace

In John 4 we find ourselves at an intersection where a beautiful collision will soon take place. Jesus is traveling on his way to another city. John tells us in John 4:4 that "he had to go through Samaria." That seems like a strange way to put it. At the time,

Jews would go out of their way to not go through Samaria. They would typically go around it and try to steer clear of any Samaritans. There was a lot of prejudice and hatred between the Jews and the Samaritans. They tried hard to have nothing to do with each other, to the point that if a first-century Jewish person read this, he would think John was making the point that Jesus *had* to go through Samaria because he had no other choice. Maybe a road was closed or traffic was backed up from so many people going around Samaria that he *had* to go through it.

Imagine if you asked a husband, "What did you do on your date last night?" He's not going to simply say, "I went to Yankee Candle and smelled candles." That would be awkward for everyone. If he admits to it at all, he's more likely to say, "I had to go to Yankee Candle and smell the different candles." The phrase *had to go* is important. He's making it clear that he was going against his will. He didn't have an option. He was forced into it. That's how a Jewish reader of the time would have heard this, but as you and I read the story, it seems clear that Jesus wasn't *forced* to go to Samaria, as if Jesus could be forced into anything.

Instead it seems like Jesus went out of his way to go to Samaria. "Had to go" seems to be used more in the sense that he had an appointment he had to keep. Like he looked on the calendar that was established before the creation of the world and saw he was supposed to be at a specific place at a specific time to meet a specific person. There was going to be a beautiful collision and God had it circled on his calendar. Grace chased this woman down and caught up with her at a well outside of town.

Jesus *had to go* to Samaria. He arrives around noon, in the heat of the day. He comes to the well and sits down to rest while his disciples go into town and get some food. It's an unusual time and place to meet someone. People would come to the well in the morning hours or in the late evening, not at noon when the sun was beating down. But then he sees the person he is waiting on. A woman arrives at the well to get some water. It was an unusual time for such a chore, but it was also uncommon that she was alone. In those days women would go to the well together, in the same way that women today are rarely seen going into a restroom alone.

What we soon discover is.that this woman has a rough past and a bad reputation. It's hard to say if the reason she's alone is because she avoided people or they avoided her. It was probably mutual. She had grown tired of the judgmental looks and the whispers behind her back. So she went by herself, with only her shame and rejection to keep her company.

When she arrives, Jesus asks her for a drink, and she's not sure how to respond. She's taken aback that he, a Jewish man, would speak to her, a Samaritan woman, and she calls him on it.

> "You are a Jew and I am a Samaritan woman. How can you ask me for a drink?" . . . Jesus answered her, "If you knew the gift of God and who it is that asks you for a drink, you would have asked him and he would have given you living water." (vv. 9–10)

Now she's really confused. She's thinking in terms of physical water for her physical thirst, so she points out that Jesus doesn't even have a bucket to draw water with. And Jesus explains to her that he is the living water, and that if she drinks this water she'll never thirst again.

She's still not exploring the metaphor. He's not making sense to her. So Jesus decides to be a little more direct with her.

> He told her, "Go, call your husband and come back."
> "I have no husband," she replied.

Jesus said to her, "You are right when you say you have no husband. The fact is, you have had five husbands, and the man you now have is not your husband. What you have just said is quite true." (vv. 16–18)

Well, that's uncomfortable. I think at this point she might be ready to go back to talking in metaphors. Jesus doesn't step away from the truth. He describes the reality of what she's done and the mess that her life has become. The well of relationships that she keeps drawing from isn't quenching her thirst, and Jesus isn't going to politely pretend that everything is OK when he knows that everything is not OK. If she's going to receive his grace, she needs to stop hiding in her sin.

This is hard, and I know we want to find another way, but here's the truth: before we collide with the grace of God, we must collide with the truth of our own sin. I wonder what hard truth Jesus would say to you and to me. Maybe he would say:

Your short temper keeps everyone around you on edge, and bitterness toward you is growing in your family.

Your drinking has gotten out of control. It's affecting a lot more people than just you.

Your porn problem is killing any chance of intimacy you have in your marriage.

Your flirting is leading you down a path that will devastate your family.

You're allowing your heart to fall for a girl who's causing you to fall away from me.

You're choosing your live-in boyfriend over your relationship with me. It's going to have to be one or the other.

You're going deeper into debt to feel better about yourself, but the water out of that well isn't going to satisfy you.

Your self-righteous and legalistic spirit is causing the people
at your job to stay away from me.

Your judgmental attitude and your harsh tone are costing you
a relationship with your grandkids.

Jesus speaks some difficult truths. It's the part of the collision with grace that we do our best to avoid. And like any of us
would do, the woman at the well tries to steer the conversation
away from her sin and shame.

> "Sir," the woman said, "I can see that you are a prophet. Our
> ancestors worshiped on this mountain, but you Jews claim that
> the place where we must worship is in Jerusalem." (vv. 19–20)

False Assumptions

Let's push *pause* on our story and talk about some false assumptions this woman made about Jesus. These are the same
assumptions that can cause us to miss his grace in our own lives.

Assumption #1: Jesus wants nothing to do with me.

If your assumption about Jesus is that he doesn't have any
interest in you, then there's a good chance you've never had
much interest in him. Said another way, it's not that you don't
want grace. Who wouldn't want grace? It's that you're convinced
grace doesn't want you.

Feeling rejected can be one of the worst feelings to experience. When someone experiences rejection early and often, they
quickly learn to build up walls to keep people from getting close.
Given this woman's history of husbands, she was likely careful
to avoid putting herself in a position of vulnerability. After all,

you don't run the risk of rejection if you never give someone a chance to hurt you.

But Jesus went out of his way to be with this woman. Grace chased her down because that's what grace does.

After preaching at one of our Saturday-night services, I was standing down front as we worshiped. A man came to talk to me. I could tell he had been crying and was still a little emotional. He told me his name, and I asked how I could pray for him.

He cried his way through his answer. "Well, my wife has left me. It's my fault. I've done some really stupid things. I haven't treated her the way she deserves. She tried to tell me but I just wouldn't listen. Would you pray that God would forgive me and my wife would forgive me? I know I'm ready to make some changes, but I'm not sure that God would want me here after the mess I've made of things."

He was assuming that his mistakes were greater than God's grace and that Jesus wouldn't want anything to do with him. I prayed for him and asked God to intervene in his marriage. I prayed that God would draw him and his wife back together again. I asked God to fight for him and for his marriage. But more than anything, I prayed for his relationship with Jesus, that he would know it wasn't an accident he was in church and that God wasn't rejecting him but was ready to help him.

After I prayed I asked him if this was where he went to church. He explained, or rather confessed, that he hadn't been to church since he was a kid. I said, "Oh, does your wife go here?" He explained that she didn't go to church either. Then I asked him what made him come and he said, "I don't know. I was driving by and just felt like I *had to go.*"

I think I understood what he meant. I connected him to a man who presented the gospel to him, prayed with him, and got some information from him so we could follow up.

On Sunday morning, the very next day, I had finished with my message and was standing down front as the service was wrapping up. Two ladies came down to talk with me. It turns out they were sisters. One sister was comforting the other, who was clearly going through something difficult.

Before I had a chance to ask for her name or why she had come down, she explained, "I haven't been to church in a long time. I hope it's OK that I'm here. Last night I was so upset and my sister said I had to come this morning."

She asked me to pray for her husband, because they had recently separated. She asked if I would pray that God would soften his heart, because she didn't think he cared anymore.

At this point my heart was pounding. I said to her, "I didn't get a chance to get your name. Can you tell me your name?"

Do you ever get the feeling that God kind of winks at you?

I excitedly told her that her husband had come forward in tears just the night before. He had repented and asked God for help. I could tell she was having a hard time believing it. It was a beautiful collision, and grace was flying everywhere.

Both of them were making the assumption that God had given up on them and it was too late. They presumed that their marriage was too much of a mess, and he wouldn't want to have anything to do with it. But God made it clear that he was ready to meet them right where they were.

Assumption #2: Jesus is more interested in religion than me.

Did you notice what the woman at the well does in the conversation? She tries to distract Jesus by talking about religion. She tries to avoid this collision by engaging him in some religious argument that could be debated endlessly. These days grace often gets overlooked because the church gets caught up in religious arguments and interpretive differences.

I'm amazed at how easy it is for us to become distracted with religious or even pseudoreligious arguments. I think we are especially prone to this when what we are studying gets a little uncomfortable.

Like the woman at the well, we have a tendency to get religious when Jesus starts to get a little too personal. I run into this as a preacher so often that I've developed a bit of a theory about it. The more people obsess over issues that clearly fall under the umbrella of theological interpretation or opinion, the more likely it is they're trying to keep Jesus from getting too personal in some area of their lives.*

I used to get distracted by this quite a bit. Someone would email me and go off on some interpretative detail they felt like I missed, and I'd fire off an email and defend my interpretation, and we'd go back and forth. I don't do this much these days. I'm not saying I never do it. If you want to try it, you're welcome to, but I rarely come out to play anymore. I've learned that when someone is especially determined to talk about religion, it's often because they are desperately trying to keep Jesus from getting too personal.

The Samaritan woman falsely assumes Jesus will be more interested in religion than her, so she tries to draw Jesus into a religious debate.†

Assumption #3: He's making an offer that's too good to be true.

This woman doesn't believe in water that will forever quench her thirst. Again, consider her history. She has had all kinds of

---

*The more you don't like this theory, the more you reinforce it. Just sayin'.
†Spoiler alert: Engaging the Son of God in a theological debate is not an effective strategy.

men make her all kinds of promises and she's skeptical. She's cynical. She doesn't trust a man who seems to be promising more than he could possibly deliver.

She makes a number of false assumptions about Jesus and the gift he offers her. Those assumptions keep her from getting too close. Each assumption is like a brick in the wall that separates her from grace. And as their conversation continues she's ready to be done, so she tries to wrap it up.

> The woman said, "I know that Messiah" (called Christ) "is coming. When he comes, he will explain everything to us." (v. 25)

Don't miss the irony. She says to Jesus, *I know that when Jesus comes he'll make things clear.* And I don't know for sure, but I'm fairly certain Jesus couldn't help but give a slight smile when he said to her,

> I, the one speaking to you—I am he. (v. 26)

This is the only time in his entire life when Jesus voluntarily and candidly tells someone he is the Messiah, the Son of God. And it's to this Samaritan woman with a bad reputation who's been married five times and is now living with some other guy. How's that for grace?

Chased by Grace

When the truth about your life is hard to face, when you've made such a mess of things you don't even know where to start cleaning up, when you can't forgive yourself, and guilt and shame are your constant companions, it's hard to imagine that grace is for you. Believe me, I get it.

Some of you think that the worst thing that could happen to you is that your sins will be found out and your secrets will be exposed. You're afraid that someone's going to bring up something you did a long time ago. You don't want anyone to know, and since God already knows, you do your best to avoid him. You think the worst thing that could happen is that you get found out and are forced to confront the truth.

But that's not the worst thing. The worst thing that could happen is that you go through your life and *nobody knows*. No one ever finds out. You just carry the weight of your guilt and shame around with you everywhere. The worst thing that could happen is that you spend your life trying to outrun God because you think he's chasing you to collect what you owe—when he's really chasing you to give you what you could never afford.

> *The worst thing that could happen is that you spend your life trying to outrun God because you think he's chasing you to collect what you owe—when he's really chasing you to give you what you could never afford.*

Father and Son

My uncle Dave and his son Wes began to talk from time to time, and after a few months they decided it was time to meet. My uncle lived in Missouri and Wes lived in Virginia, so they planned to meet at my house in Kentucky. We turned it into a miniature family reunion, and my grandparents and other extended family members were all there, excited to meet Wes.

I'll never forget standing in my driveway and watching as Wes pulled up with his beautiful family and my nervous uncle started walking toward their minivan. Wes stepped out, and we all wiped away the tears as we watched a father and son embrace for the first time.

I was too far away to hear what words were exchanged, but Wes gave my uncle a gift. A little later someone told me it was a watch. My uncle was really moved by the gift, but I didn't quite understand why it meant so much to him. Don't get me wrong; the watch seemed like a thoughtful gift, but I just didn't understand why it would cause such an emotional response.

Later that day my dad brought the watch over and showed it to me. It was a nice watch, as far as watches go, but I still didn't understand. Then my dad told me to turn it over. On the back there were two words engraved. Two words that have the power to change everything.

Pure Grace

Pure Grace

The grace effect soon began to change my uncle. The weight of his shame and guilt suddenly fell from him. His hard heart became softer. Not long after this he ended a conversation we had by saying he loved me. He had never told me that before. He has become active in a church, and the pastor has become one of his good friends.

Maybe what surprises me most is that I get to tell you this story. I didn't think my uncle would be comfortable with me sharing this story with you. After all, when he worked so hard for so long to keep it a secret, I was sure he wouldn't want me to share it with the world. But I was wrong. That was exactly what he wanted. When I emailed him and asked for his blessing to share the story, here was his response:

> Please feel free to share my situation in any way that will express God's love, mercy, and amazing grace to anyone who needs it.

When I read his response, it reminded me of the change that took place in the heart of the woman at the well. Before she met Jesus, she didn't want anyone to see her. She didn't want anyone to know, and if they knew, she didn't want to know that they knew. She could never forgive herself for what she had done or the person she had become. But then her life collided with grace, and suddenly she saw things differently.

> The woman left her water jar beside the well and ran back to the village, telling everyone, "Come and see a man who told me everything I ever did! Could he possibly be the Messiah?" So the people came streaming from the village to see him. (vv. 28–30 NLT)

When God's grace and mercy collide with our shame and guilt, it's messy but it's beautiful. Jesus knows everything you ever did, but he wants to make sure you know that his grace is greater.

3

More Redemptive
Than Your Regrets

It was a Thursday night and I was lying in bed next to my wife. She had already fallen asleep but I was awake, staring at the ceiling and thinking about my sermon for the weekend. The focus of my message was on learning to live with regrets. The grip of regret can be more than demoralizing, it can be paralyzing. We can't seem to move forward because we obsess over something that has already happened, something that can't be unwound or undone. A regret tends to focus on a specific moment, a time and place where you did or didn't do something, and now you have to live with the consequences.

As I lay there thinking and praying about my sermon, I suddenly heard a crash come from our bathroom. I hopped out of bed and ran in and saw that the full-length mirror that had been hanging on our closet door had fallen off and was in pieces on the floor. When that mirror fell, it exposed something I did that I deeply regretted.

It exposed a hole in the closet door.

How did the closet door end up with a hole in it? I was afraid you'd ask that, though I suspect you could probably guess. I got into an argument with my wife. To be honest, I don't even remember what it was about.* But I got angry, lost my temper, and punched a hole in the closet door.

I really didn't want to tell you that.

The whole thing happened in a matter of seconds, but it happened.

I wish it hadn't happened.

I wish I could go back and be a patient and gentle husband.

I wish I would have responded with humility and self-control. But I didn't.

After it happened I hoped my wife would forget about it and that my kids wouldn't find out. I was afraid of what the people who listen to me preach or read my books would think of me, if they discovered what I had done. So the way I dealt with my regret was to cover up what I had done and try to forget about it. And so I went to the store and bought a long mirror and hung it on the door and pretended it never happened.

I don't know what caused the mirror to come off the door and crash into pieces. It had been there for over a year. I suppose the adhesive that was holding the mirror to the door wasn't strong enough and eventually couldn't hold it. That's a possibility, but I suspect God was listening to me pray about a sermon that would challenge people to deal with their regrets and decided to flick the mirror off the door to remind me I had some regrets

*She probably does. But I wasn't going to bring it back up.

of my own that needed to be brought out of the darkness and into the light of his healing grace.

I stood in the closet and looked at the hole in the door and then down at the broken mirror on the floor. I could see my own reflection in the broken pieces. The metaphor was hard for me to miss. I like to think of myself as a patient, kind, and humble man who doesn't take himself too seriously. That's how I see myself, and that's the image I want others to have of me—especially my wife. I bent down and started picking up the broken pieces of mirror. I couldn't help but see myself in the pieces—I wish I could go back and do it differently, but I'll forever be a husband who got mad and put his fist through a door.

The crash woke up my wife. She came into the closet and found me on my knees picking up the glass. I'm not much of a crier, but I was crying and she knew it wasn't because I was especially attached to that mirror. I'm not sure I had ever really told her I was sorry. But I was ready to repent. Through tears I told both her and God I was so sorry for what I had done. She walked over to me, and I rested my head on her stomach and cried. I felt her fingers running through my hair. Sharing my regret and repenting for what I had done, rather than covering it up or keeping it to myself, put me in a position to receive some grace, and we finished picking up the broken pieces together.

Regret vs. Shame

When we miss grace and live with guilt, that guilt usually surfaces in regret and shame. Regret and shame can, and often do, go together. They are not mutually exclusive. But there is a difference between regret and shame. Simply put, regret is feeling bad about *something you have or haven't done*, while shame is feeling bad about *who you are or how you think you're perceived* by God and others.

So in the previous chapter we spent some time getting to know the woman at the well in John 4. I'm sure she had regrets, but her real struggle was living in the shadow of her shame. It wasn't that she was trying to overcome a mistake or a poor decision, it was that her life was being defined by those things. Shame is more connected to your identity, while regret tends to be about something specific you did or did not do.

Several times a year I'll visit a prison and lead a Bible study for the inmates. I'll often stay for a while after the study to visit and pray with these men. I've learned that many of them are carrying the heavy weight of regret. It keeps them up at night. They may know that God has forgiven them, but they are constantly reliving a specific moment when they did something they never thought they would do and are consumed by what it has cost them and the people they love. As one inmate told me, "I know I have been forgiven, but I can't stop thinking about how different my life would be if only I could go back and make a different choice."

That's regret.

My guess is most of us can think of an hour or two—or maybe a decade or two—of our lives that we would give just about anything to have back. We would do things differently. In hindsight we can see the effect of that sin in our lives and in the lives of people we love. Enough of the bill has come due that we realize the cost is much more than we ever thought possible. And we never thought about the price others would have to pay.

I've noticed that when people talk to me about their regrets they typically begin the sentence with these words: *If only I . . .*

I recently came across a website called "Secret Regrets" that lists tens of thousands of posts from people expressing regret for something they did. Here are a few examples:

- "I regret when you were a baby and I was eighteen that my boyfriend was violent and I was too scared to stand up for you and me and they took you away. That was twenty years ago and I think about you every day."
- "I regret complaining about us walking too slowly and you leaning on me for balance. It was so much harder for you being handicapped. I was just a kid, and I'm sorry, Mom."
- "I regret that I never told you kids 'I love you' when you were growing up. I regret that for some reason I still can't say those words."
- "I regret that I was a self-centered mother who didn't let you help me in the kitchen because I didn't want it to get messy."

And the list goes on. Some are less specific:

- "I regret giving you my heart when all you wanted was my body."
- "I regret that I never saved any money and I'll never be able to retire."
- "I regret that I never told you how I felt."
- "I regret that I didn't fight for us."
- "I regret how much time I spent complaining and criticizing."

If there is one thing we have in common, it's that all of us have some regrets. We all wish we could go back and do some things differently.

Around three years ago I was about twenty thousand words into a book and somehow the document got corrupted. Every letter of every word on every page had been replaced by one of these: *. When I see these *, whatever these * are, I feel nauseated. I was fairly sure my publisher wasn't going to accept the book if the first four chapters were all *********. That document represented hundreds of hours of work. I was in a panic to get it back. I knew that it had been backed up recently, and I was hopeful I'd be able to recover most of my work. I got an IT guy on the phone. He told me not to worry and walked me through how to use a program on my Macbook called "Time Machine." Somehow, I assume through the combination of dark magic and a flux capacitor, I was able to go back in time on my computer to before the document was corrupted. It was like it never happened.

Wouldn't it be helpful if God equipped every human with a "Time Machine" function? How would you use it? Maybe you would go back to before you ever spoke those words to a sibling. Maybe you would go back to before you had the affair. Maybe you would go back to right before you took that first drink. Or right before you walked out on your family. Or right before you accepted your ex-boyfriend's Facebook request. Or right before you agreed to go on that first date. Or right before you walked into the abortion clinic.

You may not be locked up behind bars, but that doesn't mean you're not a prisoner. Most of us are desperate to be free from the guilt and regrets that imprison us.

Regret, Remorse, and Repentance

The Bible tells us of a night when two of the disciples did something they never thought they would do. It was the night of Jesus's arrest. Jesus had been with his disciples in the upper room. Judas left the meal to betray him. He met with Jewish officials to make final arrangements for Jesus to be handed over to them.

But Judas isn't the only disciple who will betray Jesus on this night. Jesus warned the other disciples, "This very night you will all fall away on account of me" (Matt. 26:31). When Peter heard this, he was indignant. He passionately objected, but Jesus told him, "Truly I tell you, this very night, before the rooster crows, you will disown me three times" (v. 34). And then Peter doubled down on his commitment: "Even if I have to die with you, I will never disown you" (v. 35).

The sun has gone down as Jesus leads his disciples through the streets of Jerusalem. They head out of the city through the eastern temple gate and toward the Mount of Olives. They reach an enclosed wooded area called Gethsemane. Jesus instructs his disciples to pray and then goes off by himself. He knows the horror that awaits him, and in the quietness of the night he cries out to his Dad.

Jesus must have come to the Garden of Gethsemane to pray somewhat often, because Judas knows right where to find him. He leads a group of some six hundred men into the garden to arrest Jesus. Judas has arranged a signal so that all of them would know which one was Jesus. And so he walks up to Jesus and betrays him with a kiss. The soldiers move in to arrest Jesus. The disciples are outnumbered sixty to one; they don't have a chance. But Peter grabs a butcher's knife, likely the one that had been used earlier in the evening to carve the Passover lamb, and takes a swing at the servant of the high priest. Peter tries to take off his head but manages to lop off only an ear. I'm guessing Peter had a few holes in his closet door. Jesus immediately steps in and puts a stop to what Peter is doing. He picks the ear up, disconfects it,* and reattaches it to the servant.

Once Jesus is under arrest, all but two of the disciples flee. Peter and John follow Jesus from a safe distance. At some point the two separate, and Peter waits in the courtyard of the high priest to see what will happen to Jesus. That's when a slave girl recognizes Peter and asks if he is one of the disciples. And Peter does what he promised he would never do—he denies Jesus. Then he makes his way over to a fire where he stands with a number of others trying to stay warm. Again he is recognized and again he denies even knowing Jesus.

A little later Peter is recognized a third time, and for a third time Peter denies knowing Jesus. In fact, he even swears on the penalty of hell that he doesn't know Jesus. But his swearing is interrupted by the crowing of a rooster. At that very moment Jesus is being led through the courtyard. He has been badly beaten. His face is bloodied and swollen. Luke 22:61 tells us:

> At that moment the Lord turned and looked at Peter. Suddenly, the Lord's words flashed through Peter's mind: "Before the rooster crows tomorrow morning, you will deny three times that you even know me." (NLT)

Peter comes to his senses. He realizes what he has done. The very thing he swore he would never do, he did.

> Peter left the courtyard, weeping bitterly. (v. 62 NLT)

As Jesus continues through a series of illegal and unjust trials, we're told that Judas is also filled with remorse. He's

---

*Don't recognize *disconfect*? That's because you skipped the introduction. Busted!

overwhelmed with regret and is desperate to make things right. He goes to the chief priests and elders and throws the money into the temple. "I have sinned," he confesses to them, "for I have betrayed innocent blood" (Matt. 27:4).

Both Peter and Judas are filled with guilt and regret over what they have done. If they could go back in time and undo their mistakes they would, but they can't. You can't. You did the one thing you promised yourself you would never do, and it can't be undone. Maybe you didn't do it once. Maybe you did it three times. Maybe you've lost track of how many times. Now it feels like a few days, or a few hours, or a few minutes, or maybe just a few seconds will define the rest of your life.

> *Unfortunately, when we come face-to-face with our guilt, we often do everything we can to avoid remorse.*

Our regrets should lead to remorse. That's the right response when we are confronted with our sin. God's grace won't leave you there, but that's where God's grace will most often find you. Unfortunately, when we come face-to-face with our guilt, we often do everything we can to avoid remorse.

Here are some of the common ways I see people deal with their regrets:

1. *Rationalization.* Some of the common rationalizations that I hear: "I'm not hurting anyone/I can't help the way I feel/ God made me this way/God wants me to be happy." You can always tell when someone is rationalizing because you get the feeling that they are trying to convince themselves that something is OK when they know it's not.

2. *Justification.* This usually takes the form of blaming anything or anyone but oneself. Many people deal with regret by explaining all the ways it's not their fault so it's not their responsibility. "If my parents weren't so permissive/If my parents weren't so strict/If my wife wasn't so critical/If my husband wasn't so inattentive/If my boss wasn't so unfair/If the culture wasn't so corrupt."

3. *Comparisons.* We touched on this in chapter 1, but people try to make themselves feel better about their regrets by comparing themselves to others. I think this is one of the reasons people love gossip magazines and reality TV. Nothing makes us feel like what we've done isn't that big of a deal like hearing about what other people have done. It somehow eases our regret when we can say, "Well at least I didn't _____."

4. *Distraction.* This is a big one. We never stop long enough to look at ourselves in the mirror. We never take the time to reflect upon the decisions we've made. We fill up every inch of our lives with work, relationships, and entertainment. If we ever happen to have a few spare seconds, we instinctively whip out our cell phones and play games or surf the web.

5. *Escapism.* This is a hard-core form of distraction. A person can't deal with the regret they feel so they pop a few pills, smoke some weed, get drunk, or pull out the credit card and go on a shopping spree. We self-medicate trying to treat our guilt and numb the pain of what we have done, if only for a while.

Both Peter and Judas own their mistakes. They admit where they went wrong. They allow their regrets to lead them to remorse. But they deal with their remorse differently. Judas returns the thirty pieces of silver he had taken for betraying Jesus. It's good that he tried to make things right. As much as possible, we should take responsibility for what we've done. The problem is that there is very little we can do about many of the regrets we have. That tends to be one of the most significant reasons we have such a hard time living without regrets. Judas realizes he can't undo what has been done. He can't fix things or put the pieces back together, and the Bible tells us that he went out and hanged himself (Matt. 27:5).

Judas couldn't deal with his regrets. He was convinced that his regrets were greater than God's redeeming grace. He couldn't live with the weight of what he had done, so he killed himself. Most people won't deal with their regrets by way of suicide, but I'm convinced that many people are slowly killing themselves with regret.

> *I'm convinced that many people are slowly killing themselves with regret.*

Peter, like Judas, is filled with regret, but Peter repents. Regret should lead to remorse, and *remorse should lead to repentance*. I don't want to read too much into this, but in my mind it's significant that both Peter and Judas are filled with remorse, but we read that only Peter wept. The Message paraphrases Luke 22:62 as, "He went out and cried and cried and cried." Maybe the reason this catches my attention is because I have learned to look for tears as a sign of repentance. It's one of the questions I ask men who come and confess a sin: "Have you cried about it?" Maybe it seems like an odd question, but in my experience tears can have incredible healing power when it comes to dealing with our regrets. John Chrysostom put it this way: "The fire of sin is intense, but it is put out by a small amount of tears, for the tear puts out a furnace of faults and cleans our wounds of sins."

Second Corinthians 7:10 makes a possible distinction between the way Judas and Peter dealt with their regrets: "Godly sorrow brings repentance that leads to salvation and *leaves no regret*, but worldly sorrow brings death" (emphasis added).

One early morning, after Jesus had risen from the dead, Peter was out with some of the other disciples fishing. This is what he did for a living before he became a full-time follower of Jesus. Maybe he had returned to the business feeling like a failure after denying the one he had left everything to follow. Maybe he had repented of his sin and been forgiven but would be forced to live the rest of his life with his regrets—thinking of what could have been and how God might have used him, if only . . .

From the boat Peter saw a lone figure walking on the shore about a hundred yards away. The man called out to the boat, "Have you caught anything?" Peter and the others responded, "No, nothing." The man on the shore said, "Throw your nets on the other side." The fishermen complied and their nets were full of fish (see John 21:4–6).

Peter realized it was Jesus, and he couldn't wait for the boat to get back to shore. He dove into the water and swam to him. Jesus was cooking breakfast, and they gathered around a charcoal fire. Have you ever noticed how a distinctive smell can bring back a memory? The stench of a locker room reminds you of football, the peculiar odor of a factory reminds you of a summer job, a distinctive perfume can remind you of your first date with your wife. I wonder if the smell of those coals triggered in

Peter's mind the last time he had stood around a fire—when he had denied Jesus.

As they stood around that fire, three times Jesus asked Peter, "Do you love me?" Three times Peter affirmed his love. Then Jesus said, "Feed my sheep" (see vv. 15–17). Jesus is telling Peter that he doesn't have to be imprisoned by his regrets. Jesus still has a great plan for Peter. Grace has the power to redeem regret.

A Trophy of God's Grace

The morning after we picked up the broken pieces of the mirror that had fallen off the closet, I told my wife that I was feeling like God wanted me to share with the church the story of me punching a hole in the door and then covering it up. I asked her if she was OK with that. I realized that the story would be embarrassing for her. She might not want thousands of people to know that she's married to a guy who punched a hole in her closet door. I was secretly hoping she would say no, because I was sure God would understand and let me off the hook.

But when I asked for her permission, she said, "If you think that's what God wants you to do, then you should."

I told her the truth. "I'm just a little afraid of what people might think of me." With a little laugh, she replied, "Trust me, we're not the only ones with a hole in our door."

That weekend I stood up to talk about the difference between living with regrets and repenting so that we can be set free by grace. I came clean and told the church that their preacher had lost his temper and punched a hole in the door. When the service was over I saw one of our church leaders walking over to me. I looked down as he approached. I was embarrassed and not sure what he was going to say. He gave me a hug and said,

"No one knows this, but there's a hole behind a picture in my bedroom." We talked for a few minutes, and by the time we were finished I looked up to see five more guys waiting to talk to me. You'll never guess what they wanted to tell me. When my wife said we weren't the only ones with a hole in our door, I assumed she meant that metaphorically, but after every service that weekend I had men lining up to tell me about a literal hole.

If you come to my house today and walk into my closet, you will still find a hole in the door. I never replaced the door. I didn't cover it back up with another mirror. I decided to leave it exposed because a strange thing happened. That hole in the door, which I wanted to hide because it reminded me of something I regretted, started to remind me of how much I am loved. A busted closet door became a trophy of God's grace.

Grace is greater than a hole in my closet door.

PART 2

Grace Is Greater . . .
Than Your Hurts

More Healing Than Your Wounds

My wife is an organized person who enjoys making lists, creating systems, and putting things in their right place. These are concepts I'm only vaguely familiar with. I'm as adept at organization as I am at performing septal myectomy surgery. And in case there is any confusion, I'm not adept at that at all.

She has recently been reading a book called *The Life-Changing Magic of Tidying Up*. The subtitle is *The Japanese Art of Decluttering and Organizing*. So the premise of this book is that "tidying up" is "life-changing magic" and that "decluttering and organizing" is an "art." This is not the kind of propaganda I want in my house.*

My wife was going through this book both by reading it and by listening to the audio version. One day I came home

*It should be noted that *decluttering* is not an actual word, thus invalidating the entire concept.

early from work and she had the audio version playing in the house. Immediately it felt like a setup. I found out she was listening to it while she was cleaning out her closet. I pointed out to her that her closet was already annoyingly clean and nauseatingly organized. She reminded me that I wasn't allowed in her closet and then explained to me that this was a whole other level of cleaning and organizing her closet. She had gathered every item she owned into a large pile in the middle of our bedroom.

I listened to the author, Marie Kondo, explain that the key to cleaning out your closet is knowing exactly what you want to keep and then getting rid of everything else. That seems obvious enough. But she also explained how you make such difficult decisions. The trick is to pick up each and every item, one at a time, and ask each item, "Do you spark joy?" If it does, you keep it. If not, you get rid of it.

I couldn't help but laugh at the thought of going through *my* closet, taking each item in my hand, and asking, "Do you spark joy?" My wife noticed and said, "Don't laugh. Your closet is next." That threat didn't scare me because I knew she lacked the emotional fortitude to even look in my closet. I explained to her that if I tried that approach in my closet, there would be nothing left but boxers and V-necks.*

I was preparing to write this chapter, and listening to that audiobook made me think about how we become attached to emotions like anger and resentment. We store them in the closet of our hearts even though they don't bring us joy and instead rob

---

*And I'm not even sure about the V-necks. Applying the book might lead me to "The Life-Changing Magic of Wearing Only Boxers," which would then lead to "The Life-Changing Magic of Being Fired from Your Job and Humiliating Your Kids."

us of peace. Still, we just can't seem to let them go. And over the years our anger and resentment start to pile up.

It's time to clean out our closets. For most of us, there is a lot we need to get rid of. For example:

> Get rid of all bitterness, rage and anger, brawling and slander, along with every form of malice. (Eph. 4:31)

Don't you wish it was as easy as that verse makes it sound? But getting rid of bitterness and anger can be painful. It's easier just to shut the closet door, pretend everything is fine, and open it only when absolutely necessary.

In this section I want to invite you to clean out your closet and deal with some of the hurts other people have caused you. In my personal experience, and in my twenty-plus years as a pastor, I've discovered that extending grace and forgiveness to someone who doesn't deserve it and can't make it right is more than a decision we make, it's a journey we take.

Beginning the Grace Journey

The first step is to decide it's a journey you want to make or at least are willing to try. There is no magic *grace* button we can push that erases the painful memories or heals the festering wounds that others have caused us, but the difficult journey begins with a willingness to forgive even if forgiveness seems like too much to ask.

For many of you who have been deeply hurt by someone else, it's not that you want to continue living with those wounds or carrying the weight of that bitterness. It's that giving grace doesn't feel like an option. Maybe you would put it this way: "I've been hurt too badly."

I've heard many versions of that sentiment:

"You don't know what I've been through."

"Not after what she's done to me."

"He has destroyed my life."

"It's too painful to even think about."

Maybe that's you. Maybe you've done that math and reached the conclusion that the hurt done to you is greater than the grace you are able to give.

A few days after I preached on this subject at church, I received an email from a lady who is now in her midfifties. She got married when she was nineteen years old to a man who was physically and verbally abusive. As she told me some of the horrors of her story, I found myself wishing for a baseball bat and five minutes alone with this man. She was married to him for twelve years before she finally escaped. For the past several decades she had been consumed with bitterness, anger, and rage. Not because she wanted to be, but because after what she had been through, it seemed her only option. In her email she explained to me what she felt like as she listened to my sermon challenging her to open up her closet and deal with what was inside.

> I wake up every day and feel like my hate for him is going to suffocate me. I never considered that anything other than that was possible, not after what he did to me. There was so much pain for so long that my bitterness left no room for even the possibility of grace. Because it seemed impossible I had never thought about whether I wanted to forgive him or not. As I listened to your sermon, I was overcome by the realization that I had never even tried to forgive. In fact, I had never even considered that God would want me to. I still don't know if it's possible, but I'm ready to at least try.

That's the first step of this journey: a willingness to forgive even if it doesn't seem possible to make the equation work.

This might be a good place for me to push *pause* and point out that sometimes there is a need to make sure the hurt is significant enough to warrant forgiveness. Sometimes we think we need to forgive someone when in reality we had no business being hurt in the first place.

My fifth-grade son is playing basketball in a league where the teams are named after college teams. He was pretty excited about what his team name might be. Would he be on the Spartans or Trojans or Lions? Actually, he ended up on the Banana Slugs. This was *not* what he was hoping for. I did some research. It turns out a banana slug is a yellow, slimy mollusk. It does not have vicious teeth or deadly poison or razor-sharp talons. It's just very slimy, and very slow.* It felt to my son like a cruel joke. Hearing the crowd chant, "I say Banana; you say Slugs!" didn't inspire him. Yesterday he played a team called the "Spartan Warriors." When you're a Banana Slug taking on a Spartan Warrior, it's hard not to be bitter. It's hard not to feel like the other team has some sort of unfair psychological advantage.

As I tried to encourage him, I was reminded of a Little League team I played on when I was his age. Our team name was "Snodgrass Bug and Body." It was a body shop in town that specialized in VW Bugs. I remember having tears in my eyes

---

*The banana slug is the unofficial mascot for the UC Santa Cruz coed teams, so it did technically qualify. In 2009 *Time* magazine published an article called "The Top Ten Worst Team Names of All Time." Number one on their list, narrowly beating out the Long Beach State Dirt Bags, was the Banana Slugs.

when I learned I would be on Snodgrass Bug and Body. My parents saw my reaction and started laughing. And pretty soon I saw the humor in it as well. We had fun making up cheers for Snodgrass Bug and Body, and we're having fun making up cheers for the Banana Slugs too. We could choose to let that name ruin our day, to be bitter, but it's not worth it. Proverbs 19:11 says, "It is to one's glory to overlook an offense." Sometimes we get dinged, in a pretty insignificant way, and we need to choose not to be offended.

Do the Math

In Matthew 18 Jesus tells the story of the unmerciful servant to help us understand not just the greatness of the grace we have received but the greatness of the grace we are to give. We discover in this parable that grace is only grace if it goes both ways. Grace is a two-way street. Receiving it from God but refusing to give it to others isn't an option. Grace flows.

> *Grace is only grace if it goes both ways. Receiving it from God but refusing to give it to others isn't an option.*

I'll say it in a way that might make you more uncomfortable: the litmus test for the reality of grace you have received from God is the extent to which you give grace and offer forgiveness to the person who's hurt you the most and deserves it the least.

Peter comes to Jesus in Matthew 18 with a question. It's a generic question, but I bet there was a specific issue that motivated it: "Lord, how many times shall I forgive my brother or sister who sins against me? Up to seven times?" (Matt. 18:21).

Peter presents a math problem, an equation to solve. Is grace greater than an offense that has been repeated over and over? It looks something like this:

$$G >/< O \times 7$$

How many times does Peter have to forgive a person who hurts him? He even makes a guess at the right answer, seven, and probably thinks he's being very gracious. Jewish rabbis taught that you should forgive someone three times; the fourth time you didn't have to forgive them. So when Peter throws out the number seven I imagine he's expecting Jesus to commend his star pupil. "Peter! Seven times? That's incredibly gracious. Why can't all the disciples be like you!?"

Perhaps Peter had someone in mind when he asked this question. Maybe he thought he'd already been gracious enough with this person. After all, he had forgiven him or her somewhere around, I'm just guessing here . . . seven times. Someone had hurt him—not once, not twice, but seven times. Peter is ready to be done. He's been hurt too badly, too many times.

Perhaps for you it's not a number of times but rather the *degree* of the offense. Maybe the person hurt you only one time, but the pain was *times* seven or even pain to the seventh power.

We don't know who Peter is talking about specifically, but I think it's safe to assume he or she is someone he knows quite well. We'll explore this more in a later chapter, but the truth is those closest to us are in a position to inflict the deepest wounds.

Last year, after I preached on forgiveness, I challenged people not just to forgive but to ask for forgiveness. After the service a man I didn't know came to apologize to me for an email he had sent me a number of months earlier where he had, apparently, said some hurtful things to me. I could tell he genuinely felt bad and needed to tell me he was sorry. His apology was humble and heartfelt and I appreciated it. "I feel terrible and I'm sorry that my words hurt you," he said. I thanked him for that and forgave him, but I also said, "Hey, I've got good news for you. I'm only vaguely aware of what you're talking about. I kind of remember getting the email you described. But bro—I went home that day, kissed my wife, played with my kids, slept like a baby, and didn't think much more about it."

I wasn't angry or bitter toward him. Why? Because I didn't know him and he didn't know me, and there's no way I'm going to give someone who doesn't even know me that kind of power over my life. Most often it's the people we know the best and love the most who have the power to hurt us.

There are exceptions, of course. You may have had someone come into your life just long enough to bring about life-altering devastation. But for most of us, the people we love most dearly are the people who have the power to hurt us most severely. The people we give our hearts to are the most likely to break them.

I'm convinced this is not a random theological question from Peter. There is a face and a story behind it. Maybe when you hear his question, a face comes to mind with a story you would do anything to forget but can't help remember. And maybe Peter's question is one you would like to ask too. "Yeah, Jesus, how far is too far? How much is too much? When is the hurt that has been done to me greater than the grace you want me to give? When does grace run out?" I don't know what word you would choose to fill in the blank of the equation below, but maybe when you do the math this is the equation you come up with:

$$\underline{\hspace{2cm}} > \text{Grace}$$

Jesus answers Peter's question, "I tell you, not seven times, but seventy-seven times" (v. 22). Some translations say, "seventy times seven." It's not that Jesus is saying 77 times or even 490 times. He's pointing to the chalkboard and saying, "Grace is always greater."

Let me pause here and acknowledge that some of you may be feeling a bit defensive. I don't mean to sound dismissive. I don't know what was done to you. I don't understand the depth of the betrayal or the degree of pain you experienced. I don't know the nightmares that wake you up at night. But I know this: grace is greater.

Maybe you're willing to accept this on some level intellectually. You want to believe grace is greater, but *emotionally* the equation just doesn't work for you. The abuse or the abandonment was too painful, and as much as you want the remaining infection of bitterness gone, it just doesn't feel like forgiveness is possible. My question is: *Are you at least willing to try?*

Grace Received

Jesus understands how difficult this equation can be, so he tells a parable that helps motivate our willingness to try.

> Therefore, the kingdom of heaven is like a king who wanted to settle accounts with his servants. (Matt. 18:23)

We're introduced to this high-powered CEO-type who decides it's time to collect from those who owe him. He takes a look at the books, and we're told that a man who owed "ten thousand bags of gold was brought to him" (v. 24). I don't know how many bags of gold you have, but that's a lot of gold. It's roughly the equivalent of $150 million today. In Jesus's day it might have been about ten times the national budget. It was an astronomical figure that probably had his audience chuckling. No master would ever loan this amount of money, and no servant would ever be able to pay it back. Jesus uses hyperbole here to make the point that this is a debt the man would never be able to repay.

Jesus continues,

> Since he was not able to pay, the master ordered that he and his wife and his children and all that he had be sold to repay the debt. (v. 25)

The master realizes this guy will never be able to pay him back, so he decides to auction off everything the debtor owns and to sell the debtor along with his family into slave labor. This wasn't unfair. In fact, this kind of treatment was expected for any debt that could not be repaid.

This parable is meant to reflect our standing with God. We are called in to give an account. He has been keeping track and we are all guilty. We have sinned and racked up a debt we can never repay.

You can live in denial and pretend you don't owe God anything. You can justify the debt or dismiss it by comparing it to others. Or perhaps you accept that you owe a huge debt and decide you are somehow going to work it off. The problem is you can't. The debt is too big. You owe too much. There is no amount of good deeds or benevolent acts that will somehow get you back to even. There is nothing you can say or do that will make things right.

Jesus begins this parable with an image of God opening up his books and calling us in to give an account. It's a reminder that apart from Jesus we are all in deep debt to God because of our sin.

Hebrews 4:13 teaches us, "Nothing in all creation is hidden from God's sight. Everything is uncovered and laid bare before the eyes of him to whom we must give account." Your teacher may not know you plagiarized the paper in college, but God knows. Your husband may not know about your flirting at the gym, but God saw it. You may have deleted the history on your computer, but God knows the websites you visit. No one else may know about your drinking problem, but he knows. The windows on the house may be shut tightly enough that the neighbors can't hear you yelling, but God can hear it from heaven. The boss may not know about the embezzling, but God knows. He knows about all of it. He even knows about the pride some of you have right now because I couldn't think of an example that applied to you.

The servant in Jesus's story is confronted with this huge debt he owes and realizes what he deserves.

> The servant fell on his knees before him. "Be patient with me," he begged, "and I will pay back everything" (Matt. 18:26).

The master knows that will never happen. There's no chance this servant will ever be able to repay the debt. But incredibly the master takes pity on him, and in verse 27 Jesus tells us the master cancels the debt and lets him go.

There are two verbs used here. One is translated "cancel the debt" and the other is "let him go." Both of these verbs could accurately be translated "to forgive."

The servant owes $150 million but the master erases it from the books. It's an incredible act of grace. The master doesn't extend the note or lower the monthly payments. He completely deletes it from the record. As significant as the debt was, the master's grace was greater.

Community of Grace

Then this parable takes a disturbing turn.

> But when that servant went out, he found one of his fellow servants who owed him a hundred silver coins. He grabbed him and began to choke him. "Pay back what you owe me!" he demanded. (v. 28)

The servant who was forgiven a $150 million debt finds a coworker who owes him about 20 bucks. He begins to choke him and demand repayment.

> His fellow servant fell to his knees and begged him, "Be patient with me, and I will pay it back." (v. 29)

That is *exactly* what the first servant had said to the master. Don't miss this: he is being asked for the same grace he received, only to a much lesser degree.

If you've never heard this story, what do you think will happen? Of course he's going to forgive him. He was just forgiven a huge debt. Of course he's going to show the same mercy. How could he not?

> But he refused. Instead, he went off and had the man thrown into prison until he could pay the debt. (v. 30)

The next detail in the story is easy to miss, but we can't overlook what happens:

When the other servants saw what had happened, they were outraged and went and told their master everything that had happened. (v. 31)

The "other servants" of the master are the ones who report the unforgiving servant to the master. They saw how much grace had been received and that this guy refused to give it, and they were outraged. Why? It was because they live in this community of grace together, with this master who doesn't treat them as servants but as sons and daughters. They have a master who is known for extravagant benevolence. So when one of their own, who has been on the receiving end of this grace, refuses to *give* grace—the community is "outraged." *Outraged* is also sometimes translated "greatly distressed" or "very sad."

That is an appropriate response when someone in a community violates the core value of the community.

Think about this a little more with me—the fellow servants become outraged when a member of their community doesn't show grace, so they tell the master on him. Don't miss this. *In the middle of this story about grace, we find a lack of grace for the person who isn't gracious.* That might seem counterintuitive, but it's not. It's why we see Jesus extend radical grace to everyone he meets who is caught in sin *except* for the Pharisees whose sin was refusing to be gracious. If grace is the core value of a community, then that community just can't ignore someone who refuses to be gracious.

Today the church is Jesus's community. And as our leader demonstrated through his actions and reinforced with his teachings, our core value is grace. Our churches should be marked by grace, flooded with grace, known for grace. So when one of our own refuses to be gracious, there should be outrage and deep sadness.

Here's my concern: often the church is known for its outrage toward people outside of our community who *need* grace rather than outrage for the people inside our community who refuse to *give it*. When we sniff legalism in our community, or see someone who has received God's incredible grace being judgmental and condemning toward those whose struggles are different than their own, we should become very distressed.

Our churches should be marked by grace, flooded with grace, known for grace.

Since grace is to be our most defining attribute, a person in a church who doesn't live a grace-giving life should shock and grieve us. Picture someone who has given his life to a peacekeeping organization using his days off to plan terrorist bombings. This may be difficult to picture because it doesn't make any sense. And if the people in one of those organizations discovered they had a member who was directly violating their core value, there would be total outrage. The person would be confronted and held accountable.

Look again at Hebrews 12:15. "See to it that no one misses the grace of God and that no bitter root grows up to cause trouble and defile many" (NIV 1984). As a community we embrace extravagant grace and we do our best to make sure that no one misses it. And when someone in our community who has received it refuses to give it, we don't just let that go.

I'm afraid this is what's happened to many people in the church over the years. Somehow, for some reason, they missed the grace of God and a bitter root began to grow. That's what happens when we talk about God and leave out grace—it creates a root of bitterness. In an earlier chapter I pointed out that in

Hebrew culture any poisonous plant was called a "bitter" plant. This not-so-subtle metaphor is making the point that a Christian or church that misses grace is *poisonous*. A root may be small and it may grow slowly, but if it carries poison it is dangerous and can defile many.

Raise a Hand

I was on Facebook not long ago and stumbled across the page of a woman who had been a couple years ahead of me in high school. There's a place on Facebook where you tell about yourself. You can put down your favorite movie, band, quote, and so forth. She had a quote from Gandhi: "I like your Christ. I do not like your Christians. Your Christians are so unlike your Christ." When I read that, it brought back a memory of when I was fifteen years old. She was probably seventeen and went to the same church I did. It was a small church in a small town, so when she got pregnant it didn't take long for the news to travel. She tried to keep coming to church, but as she began to show some of the parents started to complain that it was awkward for their kids, who really shouldn't be exposed to that at church. It didn't take long for her to get the message. *She wasn't welcome at church anymore.* And a bitter root started to grow.

The parents in that church were offended by her sin and her need for grace, but the real offense in that church was their unwillingness to give grace. Let me give you an example of how the church should respond.

I once heard a pastor named Jean Larroux talk about doing some work with a ministry called Love in Action, which is for people who are caught up in sexual addiction.[1] Jean tells about sitting in on one of the group meetings. He had never been to something like this and wasn't sure what to expect. There was a good-sized group of men who gathered together. One went to the front to share his story and talked about driving home from work and passing an adult nightclub. "I really wanted to stop," he said. When he said this a bunch of hands went up in the air. Jean didn't know what was happening. He thought, *Who would ask a question during a story like this?* The guy continued his story, "I didn't want to . . . but I pulled into the parking lot and went in." Again some of the guys in the crowd raised their hands. The man went on, "I spent the evening there . . ." and he confessed some of what he did, and again some hands went up. He said, "When I left, I felt so ashamed. I didn't think God could love me."

At this point almost every hand in the crowd except for Jean's went up in the air. He couldn't figure out what all the questions were about, and for that matter why none of the questions were being asked or answered. The director stopped to speak with him afterward. "You look troubled," he said. Jean admitted, "I am troubled. Why were there so many questions? And why didn't anyone try to answer them?"

The director said, "Oh, no, you don't understand. We have one rule at Love in Action—you never struggle alone. So if you have ever struggled with the same thing that someone else is confessing, you have to raise your hand."

That needs to happen in churches, so no one misses the grace of God. *People need us to raise a hand, not point a finger.* They need to hear, "Me too. I'm broken too." That's the only response that makes sense in a community of grace filled with people who have to rely on forgiveness to get in. I realize it may seem out of place to call for outrage in a book about grace, but outrage is appropriate when someone violates the core value of a community.

Some of you have been choked by someone in the community who wanted to receive grace from the Master but refused to give it to you. So for those of you who have grown up in a community that violated this core value, I want to take a moment on behalf of the community to apologize. I actually have a list here, if you'll bear with me:

- To the pregnant young lady who graduated a few years ahead of me: I am sorry.
- To the man who was told he wasn't allowed to be a part of the community because of a divorce in his past: I am sorry.
- To the parolee who opened up about his past mistakes and was told he was no longer welcome: I am sorry.
- To the woman from the adult industry who became a part of the community in need of a hug but instead got judgmental stares: I am sorry.
- To the addict who finally was honest about his addiction but instead of support was offered shame: I am sorry.
- To the . . .

When someone in our community wants to receive grace from the Master but refuses to even attempt to give grace to someone who has hurt them, the community should be outraged and saddened.

The New Equation

And so, the master finds out that this guy who had received incredible grace was refusing to give it.

Then the master called the servant in. "You wicked servant," he said, "I canceled all that debt of yours because you begged me to. Shouldn't you have had mercy on your fellow servant just as I had on you?" In anger his master handed him over to the jailers to be tortured, until he should pay back all he owed. (Matt. 18:32–34)

I'm thinking that's going to take a long time. How long is it going to take him to earn $150 million in prison? How about . . . I'm just guessing here . . . forever? He's *never* going to pay it back. He's going to spend the rest of his existence in a cell, imprisoned by his unwillingness to give grace and shackled by the overwhelming guilt of what he's done. Do you know what that's called? It's called hell.

Oftentimes when Jesus tells a parable, the takeaway is a little vague. Sometimes he leaves it hanging for people, prompting them to ponder the meaning and implications. Sometimes it's a little ambiguous, but not here. Jesus ends this parable with this warning:

This is how my heavenly Father will treat each of you unless you forgive your brother or sister from your heart. (v. 35)

I know some of you immediately push back on that. "What? You're telling me that if I don't forgive the person who hurt me, who abused me, who betrayed me, who cheated me, who abandoned me, God won't forgive me?" No, *I'm* not saying that. I'm just telling you what Jesus said.

This wasn't the only time Jesus issued such a warning. In Matthew 6:14–15 he said, "For if you forgive other people when they sin against you, your heavenly Father will also forgive you. But if you do not forgive others their sins, your Father will not forgive your sins."

Jesus made it clear that you can't receive God's grace and then refuse to give it to others. If God's forgiven your sins, you can't continue keeping track of the sins of others. If you do, if you hold on to the bitterness, your hurt will become hatred. It will poison you, and the infection will spread, and the not-so-subtle insinuation is that it could lead you to miss out on grace altogether. So instead of holding on to the bitterness of what was done to you, hold it up, realize it's not sparking joy, and get rid of it.

I know it's not simple; it's a journey, but the journey begins with a willingness to take the first step.

I know it's not fair. That person hurt you. They owe you something. Maybe they owe you a childhood. Or a marriage. Or a lot of money. Or at least an explanation.

It's not fair to let it go. It's *grace*. And you'll never be asked to give more grace than you've already received. That's what we learn in this parable.

Jesus answers Peter's equation with an equation of his own. Jesus's equation looks like this:

$$\$150,000,000 > \$20$$

In other words, the grace you have received is greater than the grace you are being asked to give.

I hope you don't think I'm minimizing the offense of what you have to forgive. I'm not. Neither is Jesus. I realize you may have had horrible things done to you. My heart breaks trying to imagine it. I am not making light of it. I am saying that the more you understand the holiness of God and the more you understand yourself, the more you will realize how true this is.

When the gospel sinks in, it changes your equations.

Don't Call It Grace

I grew up being taught that if I hurt someone, if I was disrespectful or disobedient, my job was to "make it right." I needed to say or do something to make it right with that person. It's a good lesson to teach kids. But it developed into an unbiblical approach to forgiveness and grace, because I came to this conclusion: when someone hurts me, forgiveness happens when the person who hurt me makes it right. When they say or do something to make things right, I will forgive them. The problem is that this is *not* grace.

Besides, what do you do when you are hurt so badly nothing can be said or done to make it right? What do you do then? Some of you know exactly what I mean. You've been hurt badly enough that you are painfully aware there is nothing they could say and nothing they could do to make things right.

That was exactly the position you were in with God when he extended his grace to you through Jesus. You could do nothing. You could say nothing. When there was no possibility of you making it right, God gave his only son.

Jesus said the master *canceled* the debt. He didn't just extend the note or make it interest-only, he erased it completely. That's what God has done for us. It's not earned. When you make grace dependent on the actions of the person who hurt you, you need to find a different word because it's not *grace*. With grace, the person doesn't fix the consequences of their sin; *you* take the consequences of their sin. That's not fair. It's not right. But it is exactly what Jesus did for you.

For You > To You

So are you willing to at least open the closet door and look inside? You don't have to, but what's the alternative? You can let the root of bitterness continue to grow. You can continue trying to hurt him as much as he hurt you. You can continue to make her pay every penny she owes. But ultimately you're the one who will pay the price for your refusal to forgive.

In this story, the servant who was forgiven a debt of $150 million refused to forgive the debt of the guy who owed him 20 bucks and had him thrown in prison. What's interesting is that in the ancient world, the person who would have paid for that guy to be put in prison would have been . . . are you ready for this? The person he owed the money to. Instead of forgiving the twenty-dollar debt, he paid for the guy to be punished. Not only did refusing to forgive not get him back what he was owed but it ended up costing him even more. That's how it worked back then.

Stop thinking about what's been done to you, and start thinking about what's been done for you.

And that's *still* how it works. If you refuse to forgive and keep the person who sinned against you locked in a prison of your bitterness, guess who's paying? You are. You're the one losing sleep. You're the one whose stomach hurts. You're the one whose relationships are being infected by bitterness. You're the one whose closet is a wreck.

The master has canceled our debt, and it is time for us to let that grace flow. It's not easy, but with God it is possible.

Here's where I want to ask you to begin: stop thinking about what's been done *to* you, and start thinking about what's been done *for* you.

Every time the pain of what's been done *to* you gets triggered, intentionally start thinking about what God has done *for* you. Because what's been done for you is greater than what's been done to you.

More Freeing
Than Your Bitterness

How difficult is it to push a button on the dishwasher? My vote is "not very," but that isn't the point. What made the whole thing ironic is that I was in the middle of writing a sermon on "happiness." Let me explain.

My wife and I were on the beach in Destin, Florida . . . without the kids. A recipe for happiness if ever there was one. Paul wrote about finding joy and contentment in God from a prison cell; I wrote about it from the beach. But in my defense it was a crowded beach. We rented a condo for four days and had to check out by 10 a.m. on Friday. Before checkout the renter is asked to do a few things: strip the sheets off the bed, put all the towels in the hallway, take out the trash, and load and start the dishwasher. My wife assigned me dishwasher duty. At about 10:05 a man in his fifties and a couple of women walked into the condo, spotted me, and said, "Ummm, we are here to clean. You were supposed to be out of here by 10." I apologized, thanked them, and told them we were headed out the door. We grabbed our stuff and made our way from the third-floor condo down to the car.

Just before we reached it, the guy came out of our room and yelled down to us in the parking lot, "Hey! Thanks a lot for starting the dishwasher. There's only a few <BEEP> things you're asked to do and you couldn't bring yourself to push the <BEEP> button?"

I had just finished writing a sermon explaining that because we have God, we don't have to let our circumstances rob us of joy. So you might think I would respond humbly.

You would be wrong. Instead I thought, *Oh, you want to over-react and get sarcastic? I can speak that language.* I yelled up at him, "I'm so sorry you had to push that button. I'm sure that had to be exhausting," and then laughed condescendingly. He yelled back at me, with a few more choice words, and I yelled back at him. By now my wife is in the car with the door shut. Finally, he stormed off, still yelling. The last thing I heard is him calling me "a worthless <BEEP> of <BEEP>."

I got in the car and slammed the door.

At this point I should have held the situation in my hand, taken a look at it, realized it wasn't sparking joy, and let it go. I should've thought to myself, *Be joyful always.* I should have remembered that *love is patient and love is kind.* I should have put the car in gear and pulled out as I laughed the whole thing off. That's what I should have done.

That's *not* what I did. I sat there steaming about how I had been disrespected. I heard my wife say, "Let's just go." I might have listened, but this is a woman who paid real money for *The Life-Changing Magic of Tidying Up.* I said, "Oh, no. That man needs to hear some hard truth." I got out of the car, but before I could shut the door I heard my wife tell me, "Say a quick prayer on your way up."

I started to head up the three flights of stairs to confront Mr. "Can't push the button on the dishwasher in the condo but has plenty of energy to yell at me from the third-floor balcony." After the first flight of stairs I felt convicted and embarrassed.* By the second floor I was telling God I was sorry, and almost immediately it was impressed upon me that I needed to apologize and give the man a tip for his extra work. I opened my wallet, and all I had was a $100 bill. I thought, *Well, apparently giving the man a tip is not what God wants me to do.*

I walked into the condo, and the second he saw me he started yelling again. I could hear a voice inside of me saying, *One more round!* But even though I didn't feel like it, I said, "I want to apologize. I'm sure it's frustrating to come in and clean up after someone who doesn't do the little things. I'm sorry. I want to give this to you for the extra work you have to do and as a way to say thank you." I held out the $100 bill. Almost immediately his eyes welled up with tears. He said, "Well, I wasn't expecting that," and began to apologize. Now my eyes were filled with tears. I think we both wanted to hug it out, but instead we just shook hands.

I walked back down the steps, not feeling proud of that moment but instead brokenhearted that it had reached the point it did, and wondering in how many similar moments I had missed grace because of my pride. I began repenting of my sin to God. How many times had God wanted me to show grace and humility

*If the condo had been on the first floor that never would have happened. Thank God for stairs.

but I was too arrogant and self-righteous? I opened the car door and sat down. I was crying. Well, not crying, just teary-eyed. My wife asked, "What happened?" I told her. She patted me on the leg and said with a smile, "Oh, it's so cute. You're growing up."

It was her playful way of letting me know she was proud of me, but the truth is that when it comes to extending grace over the little things, I should've grown up a long time ago.

Growing Up

In Ephesians 4 Paul writes about the church (the "body of Christ") being "built up" (v. 12). He says we need to "become mature, attaining to the whole measure of the fullness of Christ" (v. 13). If we do that, Paul says, "we will no longer be infants," and instead "we will grow to become in every respect . . . mature" (vv. 14–16).

In this chapter of the Bible, which is all about growing up and living "a life worthy of the calling you have received" (v. 1), we find the major application is letting go of bitterness and offering forgiveness.

> "In your anger do not sin": Do not let the sun go down while you are still angry, and do not give the devil a foothold. (vv. 26–27)

> And do not grieve the Holy Spirit of God, with whom you were sealed for the day of redemption. Get rid of all bitterness, rage and anger, brawling and slander, along with every form of malice. Be kind and compassionate to one another, forgiving each other, just as in Christ God forgave you. (vv. 30–32)

Why, when we're instructed to grow up and become mature in Christ, is the emphasis placed on offering grace and forgiveness?

I think it's because *we're never more like God than when we forgive.* Here in Ephesians 4, and throughout the Bible, we see a direct connection between the grace God gives us through Jesus and the grace we're to give to each other.

Spiritually speaking, learning to forgive is growing up.

In the last chapter we saw that the first step in the journey of giving grace is a willingness to forgive because you have been forgiven. These next three chapters will lay out three significant mile markers on this journey of giving grace.

In this chapter we will focus on releasing our feelings of anger, bitterness, and rage over to God. In the next chapter we will attach a name and a face to those feelings and be challenged to release the person who hurt us over to God. And then in the final chapter of this section, chapter 7, we will address the possibility of reconciliation. It's not always possible and sometimes it's not appropriate, but when forgiveness results in reconciliation it most accurately reflects God's grace and forgiveness toward us.

> *When forgiveness results in reconciliation it most accurately reflects God's grace and forgiveness toward us.*

Our emotions can tie us up, hold us down, and have a way of choking our resolve to forgive. They are roadblocks that keep us from moving forward with forgiveness.

It's time for some of us to grow up and do what we don't feel like doing. Instead of making this journey dependent on our emotions, or relying on our own resolve, we need to ask the Holy Spirit to help us clean out our closets and finally get rid of the anger and the bitterness that have piled up and kept us from making progress.

We tend to deal with our hurts and our anger in one of three ways.

1. Repression

I started thinking about the wounds we receive in life and asked some of my Facebook friends to help me. I asked them to tell me about something they've experienced that has been difficult to forgive.

As I read through their responses, I was amazed how often I read sentences like "I've never told anyone this before," or "I've been carrying this weight too long."

Too often this is the way we deal with our hurts. Instead of surrendering them to God, we push them down and try to repress our anger. We think we are successfully dealing with our feelings by refusing to let them surface. The definition of *repress* is "to suppress something by force." So there's something that wants to come to the surface, but it's held down.

A lot of us were probably taught to deal with our emotions in this way. We don't let anyone see them. We put them in a closet and we close the door. The problem is when we repress these emotions they don't go away—they go toxic.

Have you ever watched *Deadliest Catch*? Before watching this reality show, I could never understand why Alaskan king crab cost so much. Now I do. Crab fishermen on the Bering Sea stay awake night after night, fighting against forty-foot waves and icy conditions to set seven-hundred-pound crab pots in hopes of putting an expensive dinner on your plate at the local Red Lobster.

If you've seen the show, you know there are plenty of injuries and no doctors. It turns out the Bering Sea is a breeding ground not only for crabs but also infections. In one episode, greenhorn John Walczyk injures his hand. His concerned shipmates do nothing for him other than call him a pansy and give him a hard time. Soon his hand gets infected. If you have a strong stomach, you can check it out online. If not, I'll describe it this way: the back of his hand and his middle finger were roughly the color of Pepto-Bismol and swollen like a water balloon. A water balloon filled not with water or Pepto-Bismol but with puss. Puss that was oozing out of a hole in the back of his finger. A nurse was called in to look at it and immediately told John to go to a doctor. The wound needed to be opened up, cleaned out, and then closed up so it could heal.

I've never done any crab fishing on the Bering Sea. I wouldn't spend the money to eat crabs from the Bering Sea. But as a pastor I have been called in to talk to countless people who have been hurt deeply and have lived too long with a severe infection. Often I discover the person was wounded earlier in life but ignored their emotions, so healing did not take place. The infection of bitterness set in and, untreated, has spread.

In each of these conversations I think of the verse we keep coming back to: "See to it that no one misses the grace of God and that no bitter root grows up to cause trouble and defile many" (Heb. 12:15 NIV 1984). Repressing anger leads to bitterness that can lead to missing out on the grace of God. If there is any hope for healing, we have to stop repressing our feelings, hold them up and examine them one piece at a time, and decide if we want to keep them or let them go.

How can we tell if we have repressed anger or bitterness from wounds we received? Look for these warning signs.

One is if we have become *disproportionately angry over little things*. The anger we've allowed to pile up in our closet eventually forces down the door and begins to spill out. We find ourselves feeling irritable and angry over small things. We—and those around us—see our constant irritability or our angry outbursts and think, *Where did that come from?*

It's the guy at the hotel waiting for the elevator that isn't arriving quickly enough. So he's violently pushing the arrow button as his face turns increasingly red. He starts demanding, "Where is the elevator!?" Often this guy is not just angry with the elevator. There's something under the surface. That's the thing about suppressing our anger; eventually it's going to come up. Perhaps you've experienced this. Someone cuts you off in traffic and disproportionate anger comes exploding out of you. Or you find yourself yelling at your kid because of a spilt drink. A lot of anger over a little thing might reveal repressed bitterness that has turned toxic and is seeping out.

Another indication is if we *complain about everything*. People who repress resentment over hurts they've received tend to see everything through a negative lens. They constantly complain about teachers, coworkers, neighbors, relatives, servers, and other drivers. They can find the negative in anything. Instead of seeing the world through the lens of grace, they see the world through the lens of bitterness. It can end up defining them and that type of negativity has a way of becoming self-fulfilling.

Another sign we may have repressed anger is if we're *overly sensitive and defensive*. In fact, you might be feeling a bit defensive right now reading this chapter. *Wait, it sounds like you're describing me. But I'm not overly sensitive and defensive!* Right. . . .

You might say, "I'm not overly sensitive and defensive. I know that, because no one has ever told me I'm overly sensitive or defensive." Do you know why no one has ever told you you're overly sensitive and defensive? It's because you're overly sensitive and defensive. They don't want to tell you because they don't want you to become angry. So they do their best to avoid you.

Your coworkers quickly walk past your office and pretend to be on their cell phone. Your kids come in the door from school and spend the evening in their rooms in hopes of not setting you off. Your spouse is curled up in a fetal position in the corner of the house hoping to go unnoticed and scared that you might erupt.

You may think you've kept these emotions contained in the closet, but if you find that you get disproportionately upset, have a tendency to complain, or respond defensively, then maybe some of that bitterness, rage, and anger are spilling out.

2. Rehearsal

Have you ever had a favorite movie you kept saved on your DVR* so you could watch it again and again? Maybe you watch *Elf* every Christmas season, or *Hoosiers* every basketball season, or *Revenge of the Nerds* every . . . nerd season?

What we intentionally do with our favorite movies we often unintentionally do with our least favorite memories. We keep the moment of betrayal or the hateful words or the unfair treatment cued up and ready to play. You don't repress what happened to you, you rehearse it. Rehash it. Replay it. Again and again. And it turns your hurt into resentment. You think that if you don't, you're letting the person get away with what they did—but really you're just letting them continue to hurt you.

*Or, for my readers over forty, "you kept a DVD." Or, for my readers over fifty, "you kept a VHS tape." Or, for my readers over sixty, "you kept a slide projector presentation."

You stop any healing that may have started by tearing off the scab and watching it bleed.

Remember what Paul wrote in Ephesians 4:26–27: "Do not let the sun go down while you are still angry, and do not give the devil a foothold." The anger we hold on to gives the devil a foothold in our lives. The word *foothold* captures the idea of an opportunity. Another way to think of it is, "Do not give the devil a staging ground." The idea is that when we repress or rehearse anger, we are giving the devil a place to establish a base camp from which he is able to carry out his missions. Unresolved anger is an open door the devil can walk through and use to gain access to the rest of the rooms in our house.

All kinds of health issues are connected to chronic anger, like heart disease, stroke, blood pressure, arthritis, insomnia, gastrointestinal problems, ulcers, lupus, skin problems, and sleep problems. Bitterness can create new health problems or exacerbate existing ones. The truth is these emotions not only mess with our minds but can actually threaten our lives. It's been said that not forgiving someone is like drinking poison and then waiting for the other person to die, and that may be more true than we think.

An article in the *New York Times* declared, "Researchers have gathered a wealth of data largely suggesting that chronic anger is so damaging to the body that it ranks with—or even exceeds—cigarette smoking, obesity, and a high-fat diet as a powerful risk factor for early death."[1] In a study at the University of Michigan, a group of women were tested to determine which were harboring long-term bitterness. Then all the women were tracked for eighteen years, and the outcome was startling: women with suppressed anger were three times more likely to have died during the study than those who didn't have that kind of bitter hostility.[2]

Rehearsed anger can also lead to relationship problems. Bitterness can destroy any chance we have at intimacy in marriage. Our unresolved anger toward a parent can cause us to have misplaced anger toward our spouse, or anger toward our spouse can lead to misplaced anger at our job. This is called *transference*. I think the devil came up with transference. He loves to use our anger to wreak havoc in our relationships. Or it may not be misplaced anger, it may simply be that you don't have the emotional energy you need for your relationships because you drained it all to nurse your resentment toward someone who's not even a part of your life anymore.

Rehearsed anger also does damage spiritually. In the passage in Ephesians about not sinning in our anger and getting rid of our bitterness, we're warned, "Do not grieve the Holy Spirit" (Eph. 4:30). Why would the Holy Spirit be grieved because of anger in our hearts? Because our hearts are his home.

This morning my wife called me in distress. Apparently she found mouse poop in the pantry. She is not afraid of mice. Rather, I feel confident that mice are afraid of her. These mice undoubtedly quickly realized they had the wrong address. But anyone whose recreational reading includes books like *The Life-Changing Magic of Tidying Up* is going to have a problem with mouse poop. Now, my wife would not have found it traumatizing to find mouse poop in your pantry. She was grieved—and no, that's not too strong a word—because there was mouse poop in *her* pantry.

The Holy Spirit has made his home in your heart. He is working to help grow us up. He is working to grow his fruit in our lives. Galatians 5 tells us the kind of fruit the Holy Spirit wants to grow in our hearts: love, joy, peace, patience, kindness, goodness, gentleness, faithfulness, and self-control (vv. 22–23).

But if we keep rehearsing anger, the weeds of bitterness and rage begin to grow and choke out the fruit that the Holy Spirit wants to produce in our lives.

3. Release

I know on the surface Paul's direction to "get rid of it" doesn't seem helpful. Obviously if it was just a matter of getting rid of it, we would have done that a long time ago. I don't think Paul is trying to be dismissive or simplistic but rather wants us to understand that this is the only option.

We can repress or rehearse our anger, or we can take the third option: we can release it. We'll delve deeper into this in the next chapter, but for now let me assure you that releasing it does not make light of what happened to you. It doesn't diminish the seriousness of the offense or the severity of your pain. Saying "release it" may sound simple, but releasing it is extremely difficult.* In fact, it might even be impossible on your own.

For some of you, if I were sitting across the table right now and we were having this conversation, this would be the time when you might look at me with a clenched jaw and gritted teeth and tell me that I don't know what I'm talking about, because I don't know what you've had to go through. Saying "release it" sounds fine as a general concept to dealing with anger, but when "release it" gets applied to a person's specific situation, it's easy to dismiss as simplistic and unrealistic.

So let's look at a case study in the Bible—a man named Stephen. He was an early church leader at a time when there was

---

*Like my wife telling me to release the remote control. It's not that I don't want to, it's that I'm physically incapable.

a lot of opposition to speaking about Jesus. In Acts 7 Stephen tells a huge crowd about who Jesus is and what he did for them. Here's how they responded:

> At this they covered their ears and, yelling at the top of their voices, they all rushed at him, dragged him out of the city and began to stone him. Meanwhile, the witnesses laid their coats at the feet of a young man named Saul. (vv. 57–58)

How would you react when a group of hate-filled people starts throwing rocks at you, knowing they'll continue until you're dead? Here's what Stephen did:

> While they were stoning him, Stephen prayed, "Lord Jesus, receive my spirit." Then he fell on his knees and cried out, "Lord, do not hold this sin against them." When he had said this, he fell asleep. (vv. 59–60)

Stephen prayed that God would offer his murderers grace and forgiveness. Where do you think he learned to pray like that?

When Jesus was crucified, he prayed from the cross for those who were killing him, "Father, forgive them, for they do not know what they are doing" (Luke 23:34). Jesus prayed that God would offer his murderers grace and forgiveness.

I wonder some things when I read all this.

First, I wonder if Stephen was close to the cross when Jesus died and heard him, or if maybe John told Stephen about what Jesus prayed.

Second, I wonder if Jesus and Stephen both prayed that *God* would forgive their murderers, instead of just offering forgiveness themselves, because ultimately what matters most, what people need most, is God's forgiveness, not ours.

Third, I wonder if maybe Jesus, and especially Stephen, prayed God would forgive them because in that moment they didn't have forgiveness to give. I said forgiveness isn't simple; it's difficult and maybe even impossible on our own. Perhaps Stephen couldn't muster up the grace to say, "I forgive you" to the men who were killing him, so instead he prayed that God would, which is what they really needed anyway.

When we live in grace, releasing doesn't mean giving up, it means giving it to God. When I say "release it" I'm not saying to let it go into some mystical abyss of bad feelings. It's not that you randomly or arbitrarily release it. No, you release it *to God*. You decide to let him carry the weight of what was done to you. You decide to trust him to deal with the other person. You loosen your grip from the pain of what was done to you and you place it in God's hands.

Prayer is what makes forgiveness possible—what makes the impossible possible. Jesus and Stephen didn't look their murderers in the eye and say, "I forgive you." They looked up to heaven and said, "God, forgive them." And maybe if you've struggled to forgive, this is a good place to start. Perhaps the first step isn't to go to the person and say, "I forgive you," but to pray and ask God to do what you haven't been able to do.

I mentioned asking Facebook friends to share their stories of being wounded. I was inspired by so many of them. As I read their stories I was humbled by how many times I have held tightly to my anger and refused to release it to God. Here's a comment that I hope will help you believe that you can do this:

> We had been married for almost thirteen years when his company relocated us to Baltimore, MD. I gave up my family, friends, career, and church home of more than twenty years. . . .

I knew when I arrived in Baltimore that something felt different. . . . Five months after our move I learned he had been using online pornography and that the problem went back months earlier and had become a serious addiction. I immediately prayed God would give me the words to say to him without allowing my anger and hurt in this betrayal to take hold, but my husband's response to me was callous and indifferent. I would learn in the months to follow that is a typical response for a Sexual Anorexic Sex Addict. The problem was me, because he didn't have a problem.

I sought out counseling and we attended a Weekend to Remember marriage conference, but his heart was hardened.

Six months later he left me and filed for divorce. The harder I prayed, the more God would reveal my husband's brokenness to me. The more I could understand his brokenness, the easier it was to forgive him. When I cried out, "I gave up everything for him and he doesn't care about me at all," God whispered, *I know exactly how you feel*. My husband wasn't just leaving me; he was running away from God. I was told along the way that his salvation should be more important to me than saving our marriage, so I started to pray that way.

Several months into our separation I learned of another betrayal and lie, so I called to confront him. I prayed that God would lead me in this conversation and that my words would honor God above all else. Rather than confront him I found myself forgiving him for what he was doing to my life. . . .

I continue to pray that God will pursue my ex-husband and the day will come when he truly puts Jesus on the throne of his heart. I am free of bitterness and anger by the grace of God.

You may be thinking this woman's testimony isn't overly dramatic. In fact, parts of it may seem familiar, if not from your own life then perhaps the life of someone you know. And the ending wasn't especially inspiring. They didn't get back together. He didn't repent of his sin or make things right with God. In many ways her circumstances didn't change. If anything the hurt that was done to her not only continued but intensified. And yet she still feels free of bitterness and anger.

What strikes me about this woman's story is that she mentions praying for her unfaithful husband *five times* in only seven short paragraphs. *Prayer is what makes forgiveness possible.*

> *Prayer is what makes forgiveness possible.*

She offers forgiveness when he has done nothing to deserve it and hasn't bothered to ask for it. This step of forgiveness is not dependent upon the person who hurt you to do something or say anything. It's between you and God. You release the pain to him. If this woman could do it while having her life torn apart by her husband, if Stephen could do it while being stoned to death by his enemies, and if Jesus could do it while being nailed to a tree, then you can do it too. If you ask God, he will give you the grace you need. Take your anger and rage to him in prayer. Prayer is the release valve for your feelings of bitterness and anger.

More Prevailing
Than Your Vengeance

If you're in ministry, some people won't like you. At all.

Who would've guessed you could get in trouble by talking incessantly about someone people were so desperate to get rid of that they nailed him to a cross?

It's something they don't tell you in seminary or include on church job descriptions, but it's true. I get plenty of encouragement, and I'm thankful for that, but I've also received my fair share of hate mail. A number of years ago I received an especially cruel email. It was from someone out of state who listened to my sermons online. What he wrote crossed the line from harsh critique to just hateful. Honestly, it was so extreme I found it kind of entertaining. I thought my father, who had spent most of his life in ministry as well, might also get a laugh out of it and help me keep things in perspective, so I forwarded it to him.

About ten minutes later I received an email back from my dad. Actually, he *forwarded* me an email—it was the response he had just sent to the person who wrote the hateful email to me. My dad, who is one of the kindest and gentlest men you could ever meet, took it upon himself to send a strongly worded email to this man in defense of me. Though I had not asked him to, my dad had stood up for me.

As I read my dad's email to this man I was a little embarrassed. As a grown man I didn't necessarily want my dad coming to the playground to talk to one of the mean kids. But in hindsight, I should've expected that he would be quick to defend me and want to protect me. That's what loving dads do.

But What If It's Personal?

Looking back, I realize I wasn't really offended by the hate-filled email because I didn't know the person who wrote it. It didn't make me bitter and it was easy to forgive the guy because I had no connection to him. But what about when it's personal? What do you do when someone intentionally tries to hurt you, and it's someone you know, someone you counted on, someone you trusted, someone you loved?

Let's be more specific. How do you forgive:

Your ex who has tried to make your life miserable?
The nasty neighbor who has made living in your home a nightmare?
A mom who constantly yelled at you and put you down?
Your father who seems completely oblivious to your existence?
The friend who betrayed you?

Your coworker who is cruel and manipulative?

Your spouse who cheated on you?

The relative who abused you?

Of course you're hurt. Of course you're angry. But in the Bible Paul tells us, "'In your anger do not sin': Do not let the sun go down while you are still angry" (Eph. 4:26). It's natural to get angry; sometimes it's even appropriate. But when anger turns into bitterness it becomes toxic. We need to get rid of it. After enough setting suns, those feelings can become a part of you. What was done to you begins to shape your identity. What was said to you begins to define you. We can find ourselves held prisoner not by something we did in the past but by what someone did to us.

Don't confuse simple with easy. There is nothing easy about the next steps on this journey of grace.

So it's not too difficult, at least on an intellectual level, for us to agree with Paul's direction to get rid of anger and bitterness. Of course that's the right decision. If a doctor diagnosed you with cancer, you would tell the doctor, "Get rid of it!" If you refuse to give grace, be warned that the tumor of bitterness will mutate and multiply. It's only a matter of time until the anger metastasizes into every area of your life.

In the previous chapter we talked about how we need to get rid of our anger and bitterness. That's part of the forgiveness process, but forgiveness needs to go further. It's more than just dealing with your feelings, it's forgiving someone specific. It's one thing to release some emotions that are hurting you, it's another thing to release the person who hurt you. Is there a name and a face that come to your mind?

Remember what we've said: grace flows. That's the nature of it. *If it doesn't flow, it isn't grace.* We can't keep God's grace for ourselves and refuse to give it to someone else. But, practically speaking, how do we do that? Where do we go from here? How do we actually forgive someone?

I know these answers will run the risk of sounding naïve. You may be tempted to dismiss them as too simplistic. But don't confuse simple with easy. There is nothing easy about the next steps on this journey of grace.

Acknowledge It

For all his talk about getting rid of anger and extending forgiveness and grace, you may wonder if Paul ever had to live this out in real life. It's easy to pass on pious-sounding platitudes about forgiveness . . . if you've never had to really forgive anyone. Maybe that's the deal with Paul. Maybe he doesn't really know what he's talking about because he's never had to do it. It's hard to take someone like that seriously.

No, Paul had people who intentionally hurt him. He was on the receiving end of more than just an occasional harshly worded email. There are a number of examples of people causing him pain, but there are two I especially want to point out.

Some of the books Paul wrote in the Bible were to churches. For example, in the last few chapters we have been looking at a letter Paul wrote to the church in the city of Ephesus (modern-day Turkey) that is called Ephesians. There are other books in the New Testament that Paul wrote to specific church leaders. Sometimes it's helpful to match up a letter Paul wrote to a church with a letter he wrote to the leader of that church. In this case, 1 and 2 Timothy are the letters Paul wrote to Timothy, who was the leader of the church in Ephesus.

In 2 Timothy Paul writes about a guy named Alexander who had caused him some pain. He doesn't go into detail but simply says, "Alexander the coppersmith did me much harm" (2 Tim. 4:14 NLT). Another translation puts it, "He did great evil against me." Paul doesn't get caught up in recounting and complaining about everything that was done to him, but one thing we learn from him here is that you have to acknowledge you're hurt.

Sometimes we pretend nothing happened, seeking to sweep the hurt under the rug. That doesn't work. You cannot forgive what you refuse to acknowledge.

Release My Rights

Once I acknowledge what has been done to me, my first instinct is to do something in return. I need to even the score. I have a right to retaliate. I have a right to retribution. I have a right to take revenge. I acknowledge the deficit and now I'm ready to collect. That seems like the next step in getting over the hurt someone has caused.

After acknowledging the great harm that Alexander did to him, Paul continues, "but the Lord will judge him for what he has done" (v. 14 NLT).

Paul doesn't minimize the hurt that was done to him. He simply releases his right to take revenge. He's signing a waiver on his right to retaliate. This is different than releasing his feelings of anger and rage; he's releasing the offender over to God.

There's something within us that thinks, *I'll forgive when I get even. When I make them feel the way they made me feel, I can forgive.* But that's *not* forgiveness, that's revenge. The Bible says in Romans 12:19, "Do not take revenge . . . but leave room for God's wrath, for it is written: 'It is mine to avenge; I will repay,' says the Lord." Justice is God's job. When we insist on holding on to our right to get even, we put ourselves in God's place. It's a way of saying, "God, I don't think you can handle this. I don't trust you to take care of me. So I am going to deal with this situation myself."

Reading that verse in Romans 12 reminds me of my dad's response to the guy who sent me the hate-filled email. In a sense I released the critic's email to my father and left room for his wrath. He read it and said, "It is mine to avenge; I will repay." I didn't even want him to do that, but as a loving father he couldn't help himself.

In the last chapter I mentioned how we can keep playing back the episode of what was done to us, like a favorite movie recorded on our DVR. The problem is that with each playback the weight of what was done to us increases. There comes a point when we have to decide, "The weight is too heavy for me to carry. I'm not going to let what that person did to me continue to wear me down. So, God, I release it to you." We're not just releasing the pain of what was done but also releasing the person who did it.

I do want you to notice why Paul is writing about this hurtful man to Timothy. Paul writes in the next verse, "Be careful of him, for he fought against everything we said" (2 Tim. 4:15 NLT). Paul has released his rights but he's protective of Timothy. He may forgive Alexander but he doesn't trust him. Forgiveness doesn't necessarily equate to trust. Just because you give up your right to take revenge doesn't mean that the person doesn't need to be held accountable. If a crime was committed against you, this doesn't mean you don't report it. It doesn't mean the person doesn't need to answer to the law. It also doesn't mean you move forward and trust the person as if nothing happened. It may be that you need to put up some wise boundaries moving into the future. Paul acknowledges what was done and releases it to God, but then sets up some appropriate boundaries to prevent future harm. We may need to do the same.

Pray for Your Enemies

Paul then goes on to give another example of when he has been hurt. He writes, "The first time I was brought before the judge, no one came with me. Everyone abandoned me" (v. 16 NLT). Again, Paul acknowledges the offense. Paul is likely talking here about a trial when he had to stand in front of the Roman authorities. Nero, the Roman emperor, was doing everything he could to destroy the church and put an end to Christianity. Paul is referencing a trial where his life was literally on the line. In that moment of need, no one showed up. He had loved and served and poured his life into people, and none of them came to support him.

Maybe you know what that's like. You know the pain of counting on someone who let you down. You trusted your heart with someone, and they gave it back to you in little pieces. This is a different kind of hurt, because it comes from someone you trust.

With Paul, I get the sense that he wasn't especially close to Alexander the coppersmith.* But the people who didn't show up at his trial were friends he was close to and cared about.

---

*Part of the reason I assume that is because he tells Alexander's job title with his name. I don't do that with any of my close friends. I have never told my wife, "Honey, I was talking to Nathan the insurance salesman and Amy the second-grade teacher and invited them to come over on Memorial Day."

And the more intimate the relationship, the more devastating the hurt can be.

I mentioned that as I prepared for this book I asked my Facebook friends to share with me their stories of forgiving someone who hurt them. There were dozens and dozens of stories from people who were betrayed by someone they trusted, but there was one story that was different. It wasn't from the person who was betrayed, it was from the person who did the betraying. Here's her story:

> I grew up in the church. I knew what was expected of me as a moral person and as a follower of Christ. I met Bill at the park and our relationship quickly went from friendship to so much more. Our selfish desires were more detrimental due to him being married. We made attempts to be honorable and end it but selfishness prevailed. Then our secret became tangible. I was pregnant . . . a pregnancy test in my hand convicted me of my sin. I did love him, but I offered to leave the area and not disrupt his life further. I felt more culpable in our situation because I had knowingly disregarded God's voice. He made his decision to reveal the betrayal and ask for a divorce. They had been together for eight years with no children.

It turns out Bill's wife was named Lisa. Can you imagine how devastated Lisa must have been to find out her husband was cheating on her? Not only that, but this other woman would be having his baby—and on top of all of that her husband wanted a divorce. Can you imagine? Sadly, some of you don't have to.

Paul is writing about feeling betrayed. He loved and sacrificed for these people and they all deserted him. How does he feel about them now? He writes, "May it not be held against them" (v. 16). In fact, he doesn't just release his right to take revenge, he says a prayer for them, hoping that their sin won't be held against them. It's the same prayer we saw with Stephen in Acts 7, and with Jesus on the cross. It's what Jesus taught all of us to do in Luke 6:27–28: "Love your enemies, do good to those who hate you, bless those who curse you, pray for those who mistreat you."

Maybe you read that, and attach the name and face of the person who mistreated you, and it sounds impossible. "Wait, you mean I'm supposed to pray for the person who hurt me?" Yes. In fact, I'd say this will do more to get you down the path of forgiveness and grace than anything else.

***

In 1960, Ruby Bridges became the first African American to attend an all-white school. She was six years old. She was selected as one of four first-graders to integrate two elementary schools. Unfortunately, she was sent to integrate one—William Frantz Public School in Louisiana—all by herself. On her first day several hundred protestors gathered outside. She saw one carrying a black doll in a coffin. She was spit on and cursed at, and her life was threatened. She saw a doctor, Dr. Robert Coles, to help her deal with some of the pain of what she was going through. He couldn't understand how she coped so well with everything going on. He couldn't understand why she didn't seem to be angry or bitter or depressed.

One morning Ruby's teacher watched Ruby stop in front of the angry mob that was cursing at her, and she saw Ruby's lips moving. She told Dr. Coles about it. Later, when he met with Ruby again, he asked what she was saying to the crowd. Ruby said, "I wasn't talking to them. I was praying for them." Ruby later wrote in her memoir, *Through My Eyes*, "My mother and our pastor always said, 'You have to pray for your enemies and people who do you wrong,' and that's what I did."[1] Dr. Coles points out that Ruby's parents could not read or write but they taught her to do what Jesus said to do. Jesus said to pray for your enemies, so that's what she did. That's what allowed her to get rid of all bitterness, rage, and anger.

We need to do what Jesus said to do. If we're going to forgive and let grace flow, we need to pray for our enemies. You may be at a place where you won't even consider doing what Jesus said to do, but I'd encourage you to remember it's also what Jesus did for you. He prayed for the people who put him on that cross.

Lean on Him

Paul briefly shares with Timothy how he was wronged but also how God gave him the strength he needed.

> But the Lord stood with me and gave me strength so that I might preach the Good News in its entirety for all the Gentiles to hear. And he rescued me from certain death. Yes, and the Lord will deliver me from every evil attack and will bring me safely into his heavenly Kingdom. All glory to God forever and ever! Amen. (2 Tim. 4:17–18 NLT)

How do you forgive? You choose to release it, you pray for your enemy, and, I think probably most importantly, you recognize that God is standing with you—and he will have the final word.

Paul concedes that the people he was counting on let him down, and he says, "The Lord stood with me and gave me strength" (v. 17). Some of you understand what Paul is expressing. There was a time in your life when people you cared about seemed absent, but it was then that God seemed most present.

When you felt the most betrayed and abandoned, you discovered God was right there standing with you and you were able to lean on him.

Paul looks back now on the hurt that was done to him and he is able to see that God was not only with him but that God used him to preach the Good News. God brings about good from the bad that was done to Paul. It makes it easier to forgive someone when you can have confidence that what they meant for evil God can work for good.

Which reminds me . . . I was telling you about Lisa, the wife whose husband told her he was cheating, and the other woman was pregnant, and he wanted a divorce. I asked if you could imagine how devastated she must have been. Here's another question: How does a person respond to something like that? Here's how Lisa responded (remember, this came from "the other woman"):

> When Bill told Lisa of our relationship, the pregnancy, and essentially the end of her life as she knew it, she was undoubtedly devastated. Do you know what she did after she watched her life come crumbling down around her? She called me to say that she didn't hate me . . . and that while she would surely go through some tough times in the near future . . . after all was said and done . . . her prayer was that somehow we could all still be family. She later asked me if she could be Aunt Lisa to the baby.
>
> I couldn't comprehend it. All these years later, I still can't.
>
> How? Who has such strength? Who has such grace? While we certainly deserved the wrath of a woman who never deserved such treatment, after our son was born there was a friendship and true love that flowed without reserve.

Bill didn't know Jesus. He still doesn't. But Lisa and I began to pray together for him. We prayed that he would come to see the love and grace of Jesus through everything that happened.

Her grace humbles me daily. There are no words for her forgiveness. I guess the only word is *Jesus*. Her strength, her mercy, her grace are only a mere inkling of what Jesus offers.

God is standing with you and offers you a grace that is not only greater than anything you have done but greater than anything that has been done to you.

This woman, who betrayed Lisa, is right. No one has that kind of strength, that kind of grace. That didn't come from Lisa. That came from Jesus to Lisa and Lisa just let it flow.

If you have been hurt, betrayed, abandoned, or abused, God is standing with you and offers you a grace that is not only greater than anything you have done but greater than anything that has been done to you.

A Loving Father

God is a loving father you can lean on when you have no one else. No matter what you go through, you don't have to go through it alone.

OK, before I end this chapter, I have to tell you the end of the story of my dad coming to my defense and emailing the guy who had sent me the hateful email. A few hours after he forwarded me his email to this guy, my dad sent me another email. He felt bad for speaking on my behalf without my permission and wanted to apologize if he had overstepped as a father to an adult son.

Here's what he wrote:

Dear Kyle,

I wanted to apologize for responding to the man who sent you that email. I know that's not what you were wanting when you shared that with me. I am sure the reason I felt compelled to respond was because I felt the sting that he intended for you. On the rare occasion a criticism like this has been directed at me, I do much better at responding with patience and a sense of humor, but when it comes at my son, I can't help but rush to the battle line. I love who you are, son. Don't change. Keep growing. I won't respond any further and I would encourage you to let this go as well.

Love, Dad

My dad is for me. He's in my corner. If someone comes at me and my dad finds out about it, whether I like it or not, whether I'm embarrassed by it or not, they're going to have to deal with him as well. There is never any question whose side he's going to land on. He is always for me. He is always on my side.

I don't know if you have an earthly father like that, but I know you have a heavenly Father. Let him deal with your hurts. Release the person over to God and trust God to deal with the person. Lean on him. He's got your back.

More Reconciling
Than Your Resentment

Elizabeth and Frank Morris's eighteen-year-old son, Ted, was home from college for Christmas break. He had gotten a job to make a little money. It was late, and Elizabeth was worried because he was supposed to be home from work already. That's when the phone rang. Elizabeth answered and received the news no mother wants to hear. On Ted's drive home a car coming the other way had crossed the median and hit him head-on.

Tommy Pigage was driving the other car. He had been at a party where he had gotten drunk. His friends told him not to drive, but he didn't listen. He blacked out and never even saw Ted Morris's car coming down the other side of the road.

Ted died the next morning. Tommy's blood alcohol level was about three times the legal limit.

The trial was about a month later. Elizabeth and her husband were there and were enraged when Tommy pleaded innocent.

The trial was delayed repeatedly. Finally, almost two years later, the trial closed when Tommy reached a plea bargain that allowed him to be freed on probation.

Tommy was now free, and Elizabeth began having revenge fantasies in which she would kill him.[1]

Inhale, Exhale

Is grace really greater?

Is grace greater than even the pain caused by a drunk driver who kills your son?

That is what the Bible says. That is what we're saying. God's unconditional love is so transformative that the grace effect we experience will lead us to forgive even the worst of our worst enemies.

In case there is any confusion, here's what we're *not* saying. . . . We're not saying that what happened is no big deal or that healing will be immediate or that you should make excuses for what someone did to you. We're not saying abuse should be tolerated or that you shouldn't press charges if a crime has been committed. We're not saying you won't hurt anymore or that you'll be able to magically forget what happened. We're also not saying you should blindly trust someone who's hurt you.

What we are saying—actually, what the Bible is saying—is that it is possible to get rid of our bitterness, rage, and anger. The grace that flows to us through Jesus can flow from us to others. We can be set free from the prison of unforgiveness. We read in Ephesians 4:32, "Be kind and compassionate to one another, forgiving each other, just as in Christ God forgave you." We are to forgive as God has forgiven us. The forgiveness we have received from God is the motivation, the mandate, and also the model of forgiveness we are to give. Once we have received his grace we are to let it flow freely from our lives.

I have a pastor friend in Nashville named Pete Wilson. I was visiting his church recently, and he preached a sermon on how we can give the love and grace of Jesus to others. He explained it this way: "What you inhale is what you will exhale." If you're intentional to inhale God's grace and forgiveness, you will also exhale it in your relationships. But if you're breathing in anger and rage, you're going to breathe it out in your relationships.

When you're taking off on an airline flight, the flight attendant gives you a demonstration with an air mask. There's something about pulling the mask firmly toward you and covering your mouth with it. And there's something about how even if the bag doesn't in-flate, the oxygen is still flowing.* Then comes the most difficult part of the in-structions, when they tell you if you're traveling with a child to put your mask on before you help your child with their mask. As a father, if my kids can't breathe, I want to help them before I take care of myself. That's just a par-

> *As you take time to inhale the oxygen of God's grace, you'll be in a place to make sure the people around you are inhaling it as well.*

ent's natural instinct. But I realize that even though making sure I'm breathing first wouldn't be easy, it would be necessary. If I'm not breathing, I won't be any help to my child.

The same is true with breathing in the life-giving oxygen of God's grace and forgiveness and peace and joy. That's what you want for your kids. That's what you want the people you care

---

*I don't buy that. But if it keeps the nervous woman next to me from panicking, I'm fine with them continuing to say it.

about to be breathing in. But if it's not what you're inhaling, you're not going to be able to help them breathe it in either.

We need to be intentional with this, making sure we're breathing in God's grace. If you're struggling with anger and bitterness, can I encourage you to begin every day thinking about this image? As you take time to inhale the oxygen of God's grace, you'll be in a place to make sure the people around you are inhaling it as well.

As you inhale God's grace, he will teach you how he wants you to forgive others. The level of grace and forgiveness we are going to talk about in this chapter may seem impossible now, but the more his grace flows to you, the more his grace will flow from you.

Level One Forgiveness

I want you to think of forgiveness on three different levels. Let's call level one forgiveness getting rid of bitterness, anger, and rage. It's cleaning out your closet and deciding that you are no longer going to live with feelings of resentment and animosity over something that was said or done to you in the past.

It doesn't mean all those feelings will go away. Not at all. It just means that when those feelings come, you are not going to put them on and wear them around. You are going to get rid of them.

The problem with level one forgiveness is that you may never feel like forgiving someone. Maybe you've even tried to feel differently as you have read the last few chapters. You've said to yourself, *I want to forgive. I want to let go of bitterness and hatred, but I feel bitter and hateful. When I stop feeling bitter and hateful,* then *I can forgive.* Look, if you wait to forgive until you feel like forgiving, it could be awhile. If you wait to stop feeling angry and bitter until you stop feeling angry and bitter, well, good luck with that.

Getting rid of those feelings is much more a matter of obedience than most of us realize. When one of those feelings comes boiling to the surface we must hold it up, examine it, and then decide to get rid of it. Instead of continuing to replay the offense and relive the hurt, level one forgiveness is releasing that pain to God. It's making the decision to stop calling up what was done *to* us and start focusing on what was done *for* us.

Level Two Forgiveness

Level two forgiveness, which we've also talked about, isn't so much about releasing hurt as it is releasing the person who hurt you. It's choosing to write off the debt. You release your right to retaliate, and instead of seeking revenge against those who have hurt you, you begin to pray for them. It may mean accepting that you are going to have to live with the consequences of another person's sin, but you are no longer going to look to the person who hurt you to make things right or somehow pay for what they have done wrong.

There's a speaker and author you may have seen speak on TV named Joyce Meyer. In her book *Beauty for Ashes*, she shares that when she was at a very young age her father started molesting her. Soon it turned to rape. Joyce says a conservative estimate is that her father raped her more than two hundred times before she turned eighteen.

At one point she approached her mother and told her what her father was doing to her. But her mother either didn't believe her or was too afraid to do anything about it, because nothing happened, nothing changed.

When Joyce turned eighteen she moved out of her parents' house as fast as she could. She then went on a journey toward forgiveness. She had given her life to Jesus when she was nine but then basically walked away from her faith for years. As she came back to it, she realized she had to forgive her father. If she didn't, she knew what he did would continue to imprison her. At the time she had no relationship with him, but her Bible told her she had to offer him forgiveness. So, despite her feelings, she did.

When she went to him and forgave him, he didn't acknowledge that he had done anything wrong. But as much as his response upset her, she knew it didn't change what God had asked her to do.

Level Three Forgiveness

We haven't really addressed level three forgiveness yet, and some of you aren't going to like this. For some of you, level three forgiveness will seem more than unrealistic—it will seem offensive. Here's how we'll define level three forgiveness: *a willingness to be reconciled with the person who hurt you.*

Look, I realize this isn't always possible. The offender may not want reconciliation, or may no longer be living, or may not be safe for you. I also realize that certain levels of reconciliation may not be wise in certain situations. I'm not suggesting you submit yourself to further abuse. But when it's possible, level three forgiveness is the goal, because level three forgiveness is what we have received from God through Jesus.

Joyce Meyer had an evil father who abused her in the ugliest of ways, but as a follower of Jesus she knew she had to forgive him. So despite not feeling like it, she made the decision, went to her father, and offered him forgiveness. Several years later she was reading in the Bible (Luke 6) where Jesus tells us to love our enemies and *do good* to those who have hated us. Later she was praying and felt like God was saying to her, *You need to take care of your parents. You need to do good and take* good *care of your parents.* Her parents were aging and lived about two hundred miles away in a different town. Joyce had done some things through the years to help take care of them financially but felt like God was asking her to take it to a new level.

She and her husband talked, looked at their finances, and realized they had enough to buy her parents a house that was for sale about eight miles from where they lived. She realized her parents could also use a newer car and newer furniture. God had told her, *You need to take* good *care of your parents*, so she bought them the house, a car, and furniture.

Her parents thanked her, but still her dad was a bitter man, and it continued on like that for several years. Then one Thanksgiving morning, Joyce's mom called her and said, "Your father has been crying and crying all week. Will you please come over? He needs to speak to you." Joyce and her husband went over to her parents' house. Her dad confessed to her the horrible things he had done to her and apologized. He then turned to her husband and thanked him for the years of undeserved kindness he had given him.

Joyce could see there was genuine regret. She took the opportunity to explain the gospel to him again (she had done so before). She asked, "Dad, do you need to give your life to Christ?" And ten days later she baptized him in their church.

The grace Joyce showed her father may seem crazy, but how much crazier is the grace that the God of the universe has shown us? The Bible says we are to forgive as God forgave us. When

God forgave us, he didn't say, "I forgive you, but we can't have a relationship. I mean, I won't hold your sins against you, but we're not going to have anything to do with each other. You go your way, I'll go mine." No, God's forgiveness of us leads to him reconciling with us despite our sin.

In Colossians, Paul describes how God forgives us, this level three forgiveness, like this:

> For God in all his fullness was pleased to live in Christ, and through him God reconciled everything to himself. He made peace with everything in heaven and on earth. (Col. 1:19–20 NLT)

How did he do that? How did he pay for that debt to have peace?

> He made peace . . . by means of Christ's blood on the cross.
> This includes you who were once far away from God. You were his enemies, separated from him by your evil thoughts and actions. (vv. 20–21 NLT)

So we had made ourselves God's enemies and were separated from him because of our sin against him. But then comes God's level three forgiveness:

> Yet now he has reconciled you to himself through the death of Christ in his physical body. As a result, he has brought you into his own presence, and you are holy and blameless as you stand before him without a single fault. (v. 22 NLT)

God "gets rid of" your sin, reconciles you to himself, and invites you into his presence.

That's the model for how we're to offer forgiveness.

Level 2.5

About twelve years ago, an out-of-state relative of mine got into some financial trouble and reached out to me for help. It was a pretty urgent situation, and he asked us to loan him five thousand dollars.

We were in our twenties and didn't have five thousand dollars lying around the house to loan him.* But we decided to do it anyway. We pulled money out of our savings and loaned it to him. He promised to have it paid back within a year. We counted on that promise because we couldn't afford not to be paid back. We needed that money to pay some bills, our kids' school tuition, and our taxes.

The year came and went, and he did not pay it back. In fact, he never brought it up. We saw him over the holidays, and he went out of his way to avoid us. I tried to call him, but he never answered. I left messages telling him we could work out a gradual payment plan, but he wouldn't return my calls.

We ended up having to sell a vehicle and replace it with an older minivan so we could use the difference to pay our bills.

Several years went by, and I grew increasingly resentful. Having to drive an old minivan does something to a man's spirit. Every time we would see him at a family gathering and he would do his best to avoid us, I would become a little more bitter.

Eventually my wife said, "You know, I think you really need to have a relationship of some kind with him, but as long as he feels like he owes us money and as long as you are frustrated that he won't acknowledge it or pay it back, that relationship is just not going to happen." I didn't like where this was going. She continued, "I think we should forgive the debt and tell him he

---

*I know because I checked between all of our couch cushions.

doesn't owe us." I disagreed. I told her, "No, we can't do that. Even if we wanted to we couldn't do it. We need that money," and "We would just be enabling him," and "He needs to take responsibility for his decisions," and "There's no way I'm going to forgive that debt."

But we decided to forgive the debt.

I remember telling him that we wanted to forgive the debt and forget about what he owed us. We were spending time with family for the holidays again, and I asked if I could talk to him in another room. I told him he didn't need to pay back what he owed us; we were going to make it a gift, and that the debt was forgiven.

To be honest, I wanted him to be incredibly grateful. I had played the whole scene out in my mind. He would be extremely apologetic and profusely grateful. But that's not what happened. He acted like it wasn't a big deal. At first he pretended he wasn't even sure what I was talking about. He thanked me, kind of, but didn't apologize.

Over the years I've been tempted to hold it against him. Sometimes I'll think about how much money that would be now if I had invested it—$15,765.27, in case you're wondering. When I'm tempted to think that way, I have to remind myself, *Wait, I forgave that.*

A few years ago he bought a new vehicle and posted a picture of it on social media. I started to leave the comment, "Hey, that looks nice. Reminds me of this minivan I used to own . . . but *completely* different." I had to remind myself, *Wait, I forgave that. I released it. I don't replay that episode in my mind anymore.*

It's hard. People say you "forgive and forget." That's not true. You forgive and *remember*, and when you remember, you have to remind yourself, *I forgave that.*

I reconciled my relationship with my relative—kind of. True reconciliation would also require him to acknowledge that he did something wrong. Complete reconciliation is dependent on *both* parties. We could say it this way: total reconciliation requires both forgiveness from the offended and repentance from the offender.

> *Total reconciliation requires both forgiveness from the offended and repentance from the offender.*

Isn't that true in our relationship with God? He offers us forgiveness. He even made the payment required for us to be forgiven. But to be reconciled to him, we need to repent.

The person who hurt you may not repent to the degree you think he or she should. He may not realize how grievous his sin was, how much damage it caused you. She may say she's sorry, but it may seem that her level of repentance doesn't match the level of the offense. But . . . our level of repentance doesn't match the level of our offense against God.

Still, it is true that for real reconciliation to happen there must be forgiveness from the offended and repentance from the offender.

There's a story in the Bible that illustrates this. Jacob, Abraham's grandson, had a brother named Esau. A twin brother, actually. Esau was the oldest by a matter of minutes, and as the oldest he would receive his father's blessing and the birthright. Jacob cheated Esau out of these things and then ran and hid from his brother. Jacob knew he was guilty, and he knew Esau would get revenge, so he ran away. He avoided Esau for several decades. The two brothers never talked or had anything to do with each other.

Finally, there comes a point where Jacob can't avoid Esau any longer. They are going to meet, and Jacob is afraid. He receives word that Esau is coming at him with an army of four hundred men. In a desperate attempt to cut his losses, Jacob divides his family and all of his possessions into two groups in hopes that if Esau attacks one group, the other group will be spared.

Finally, the moment arrives for these two brothers to see each other again. We read, "Then Jacob went on ahead. As he approached his brother, he bowed to the ground seven times before him" (Gen. 33:3 NLT). Jacob humbles himself and shows contrition by bowing to Esau. Then, "Esau ran to meet him and embraced him, threw his arms around his neck, and kissed him. And they both wept" (v. 4 NLT).

That's level three stuff right there. *That* is reconciliation. Reconciliation requires forgiveness from the offended and repentance by the offender. It doesn't happen often, but it's a beautiful thing when it does.

On the day Jacob and Esau are reunited, one of Jacob's sons is toward the back of the caravan—just a little boy watching all of this unfold. He had probably heard of his Uncle Esau. I don't know how much he would have known about the conflict between the two brothers, but he can tell his dad is scared to meet his uncle. He knows something is about to happen. He watches his father bow down humbly, something he is not accustomed to seeing. He watches his uncle run up to embrace his dad.

This little boy, his name was Joseph, and he watched and took it all in.

Several years later Joseph had some trouble with his own brothers. They sold him into slavery. But you may remember that God worked in Joseph's life so he became the second most powerful man in Egypt. A couple decades pass, and then Joseph's brothers show up to ask him for food. There is a famine and they are desperate. They don't recognize him, but he recognizes them. If he wants it, this is his chance to get revenge.

Instead, Joseph comes up with a test to see if they really are sorry for what they've done. He wants to find out if they are repentant, and when he realizes that his brothers are sorry for what they did, this is what happened next:

> Joseph could stand it no longer. There were many people in the room, and he said to his attendants, "Out, all of you!" So he was alone with his brothers when he told them who he was. Then he broke down and wept. He wept so loudly the Egyptians could hear him, and word of it quickly carried to Pharaoh's palace. (45:1–2 NLT)

His brothers are upset and afraid, but Joseph encourages them not to be, telling them that God had taken what they meant for evil and used it to bring about good.

I feel confident that Joseph had already reached level two forgiveness, but now he's able to move to level three, and he weeps. That doesn't surprise me—when we set other people free, we end up feeling free ourselves.

And God is calling us beyond releasing our right to retaliate, beyond getting rid of our feelings of bitterness and hatred, to a willingness to be reconciled with the person who hurt us.

Grace Leads to Reconciliation

Remember Elizabeth and Frank Morris? Tommy Pigage, who was driving drunk, had killed their son, Ted. At his trial, Tommy got off on probation and Elizabeth wanted revenge.

But Elizabeth had a problem. She was the recipient of grace. A Christian, Elizabeth took her pain to God, and as she prayed she realized that her heavenly Father had also had his innocent son murdered. She knew she had to forgive Tommy as God had forgiven her.

Elizabeth went and met with Tommy. She told him she wanted to help him. Tommy came from a broken home and struggled with alcoholism. He needed help.

Not much later, Tommy got drunk and violated his parole agreement. Tommy was sentenced to three months in prison, and Elizabeth visited him regularly. When he got out, Elizabeth and Frank began building a relationship with Tommy and talking to him about Jesus. One night the Morrises and Tommy drove to their church, where Frank Morris baptized his son's killer.

The Morrises now view Tommy as their son. He attends church with them every Sunday, and then they go out for lunch. They often get together to go roller-skating or bowling. Tommy calls them every single day.

It's an amazing story that really happened. The question I have, though, is: Will it happen? Is there a reconciliation story that needs to unfold *in your life*?

Is there an enemy *you* need to forgive, to pray for, to do good to, to be reconciled with? Who is it? What do you need to do?

You can do this. Grace is greater than your hurt. Just let it flow.

PART 3

Grace Is Greater . . .
Than Your Circumstances

More Peaceful Than
Your Disappointments

I didn't know the person who submitted the request.

His name was Marcus and he was asking for financial assistance. At our church we get a lot of applications for benevolence support, but this one was unusual. He was asking for help to pay for his headstone and its inscription. I assumed we could probably say yes, but first I wanted to learn a little more. It's not every day someone asks for help to buy their own grave marker. I thought whatever words he wanted to have inscribed might tell me a little more about him. I soon had my answer. Here's what he wanted to have etched on his headstone:

Forgive Me for the Days I Wasn't Grateful

Suddenly I had a number of questions. What was he dying of? How much time did he have left? Why did he want that plea to be his legacy? And is it really a sin to be ungrateful? That seemed a little overstated. I decided to set up a meeting with him so I could explore these questions.

Sin? Really?

Before I had a chance to meet with Marcus, I found myself haunted by his desired epitaph. *Forgive me for the days I wasn't grateful?*

I started thinking about all my whining and complaining over the years. Entire stretches of my life could be labeled, "Kyle wishes things were different." I'm willing to admit this wasn't the best attitude, but was it sin? And if it was, wasn't it just a small, insignificant one?* I mean, ingratitude has to be on sin's JV team, right? Was it really something I needed to ask forgiveness for, to repent of?

I began thinking about the verse that says "Give thanks in all circumstances, for this is God's will for you in Christ Jesus" (1 Thess. 5:18). And then it hit me: this is not just a helpful suggestion or a hint for healthy living. It's a command, like "Thou shalt have no other gods before me" and "Thou shalt not kill." I'm guessing God didn't wink when he said it. He commanded it, and if we don't do it, we're disobeying him. Disobedience is sin, and sin *is* something we need to ask forgiveness for and repent of.

In Exodus 16 we see the Israelites wandering in the wilderness. God had miraculously led them out of their oppressive bondage in Egypt. Now these former slaves are making their

---

*You know, like saying Christian curse words such as "crumb," "crud," "holy crow," "dagnabbit," "cheese and crackers," and my personal favorite, "son of a biscuit eater."

way across the desert to the land God promised them, a land they could call their own. But as they make their journey, we find them complaining.

> In the desert the whole community grumbled against Moses and Aaron. The Israelites said to them, "If only we had died by the LORD's hand in Egypt! There we sat around pots of meat and ate all the food we wanted, but you have brought us out into this desert to starve this entire assembly to death." (Exod. 16:2–3)

They act like they had it so good in Egypt, like it was one never-ending fondue party. "Remember the good old days?" they pine. Yeah, except they left out one thing—the slavery part! The Israelites didn't lounge around at an all-inclusive resort. They were *slaves*.

Despite their constant complaining, God is gracious and provides food for them called manna. The word *manna* means "What is it?" or "Whatever it is." You've heard of mystery meat. This was mystery bread, and in fairness to the Israelites, "What is this?" is not usually a question we ask when something looks especially appetizing. When you sit down for a Thanksgiving dinner, you don't want to look at a dish and think, *What is it?* You don't want to point to something and say to your relative across the table, "Can you pass me . . . whatever it is?" If you're a kid, you don't want to hear your mom say, "You have to take one bite of whatever that is. I don't know what it is. Some kind of gelatin concoction your grandma made. Just put some gravy on it. Hold your nose when you swallow and you won't even taste it."*

Nevertheless, these people are starving and God miraculously provides manna. But instead of being thankful for God's

---

*Lie!

provision they complain. They don't say grace; instead they grumble. Here's how *The Message* paraphrases it:

> The riffraff among the people had a craving and soon they had the People of Israel whining, "Why can't we have meat? We ate fish in Egypt—and got it free!—to say nothing of the cucumbers and melons, the leeks and onions and garlic. But nothing tastes good out here; all we get is manna, manna, manna."*
> (Num. 11:4–6)

Well, finally, God has heard enough complaining. He gives Moses a message to share with everyone, and we discover just how seriously God takes complaining:

> Tell the people: "Consecrate yourselves in preparation for tomorrow, when you will eat meat. The LORD heard you when you wailed, 'If only we had meat to eat! We were better off in Egypt!' Now the LORD will give you meat, and you will eat it. You will not eat it for just one day, or two days, or five, ten or twenty days, but for a whole month—until it comes out of your nostrils and you loathe it—because you have rejected the LORD, who is among you, and have wailed before him, saying, 'Why did we ever leave Egypt?'" (Num. 11:18–20)

Did your mom or dad ever say, "You want to cry? I'll give you something to cry about!"? That's what's happening here. "You want meat? Oh, I'll give you meat. You'll eat meat until it's coming out of your nose."†

Their lack of gratitude isn't a wink-wink sin; it's a big deal to God. In fact, hundreds of years later, in Psalm 95, God was

---

*For the full effect, say "manna, manna, manna" with the high-pitched tone of a whiny four-year-old girl.

†In middle school this would have meant instant popularity.

still talking about the offensive, faithless complaining of the Israelites in the desert.

In fact, over a thousand years later, we read in Hebrews 3 that God was still talking about all the complaining and whining that took place in the desert.

The question is, why? Why does God take grumbling and complaining so seriously? It's because he takes it *personally*. He graciously provides for his children, but instead of noticing and being grateful, the people complain. Of course he takes that personally.

As I am a father, this characteristic of God makes sense to me. I work hard to provide for my children and make sure they are taken care of. I understand that sometimes they won't be grateful or appreciative, but when they are grumbling or complaining that can be especially frustrating.

When the Warriors were in the middle of setting the NBA record for the most wins (before a loss at the beginning of the 2016 season), I splurged and bought tickets for my son and me to watch them play the Indiana Pacers. I wanted him to remember attending a game during this historic streak. The tickets cost more than I should've paid, but it was a great memory-making night.*

But let's imagine that once we were at the game, my son says he's hungry, so I get up and get him some peanut M&Ms. Imagine that I give him the M&Ms and he takes one look and says, "I don't like peanut M&Ms! I only want plain M&Ms! I'm not going to eat these." Now imagine that he spends the rest of the game complaining about the peanut M&Ms. And says things

---

*I don't mind telling you how much I paid, but there is a decent chance my wife will read this.

like, "I don't even know why we're here; we could've stayed home and had plain M&Ms and watched the game on TV!"

That wouldn't just hurt my feelings, it would make me frustrated and angry. I'd probably tell him to shut his mouth and suck the chocolate off the peanuts. But maybe it would be a good strategy to swing by Sam's and buy a five-pound bag of plain M&Ms on the way home and tell him he's going to eat those M&Ms until they are coming out of his nose.

God has freed his people from slavery and oppression and is leading them to the Promised Land flowing with milk and honey. He has provided for all their needs so they don't have to worry about a thing. How do the people thank him? "Yeah. That's all great, God, but could you do something about the food?"

When you strip it down, complaining is a refusal to trust God and acknowledge his grace in your life.

God takes complaining personally, because complaining overlooks the greatness of the grace we have received. It undermines the Good News of the gospel and ignores the generosity and faithfulness of God. This kind of complaining is offensive to God, because at its core complaining is blasphemous. It's a way of saying, "I don't believe God is taking care of me. I don't believe he will keep his promises. I don't believe he can redeem what I'm going through." When you strip it down, complaining is a refusal to trust God and acknowledge his grace in your life.

Whining is the opposite of worship, and complaining is the rival of grace. We might flinch at that. Perhaps we'd say complaining is the opposite of thanksgiving, not grace. But grace and thanksgiving are closely related in the Bible, even intertwined. We see this in the way we talk. In fact, when we want to express thanksgiving to God before a meal, we often refer to it as "saying grace."

When we complain, we stop paying attention to what we have and become fixated on what we *don't* have. Complaining has a way of pulling the shade down on the window of grace. It keeps the light of God's grace from shining in. The Israelites ignored that they were free for the first time in generations because of their myopic obsession with what was on the dinner menu.

Grace-Colored Lenses

A while back I was at a movie theater, standing in line at the concession stand, thankful for the opportunity to spend a small fortune on some snacks. A guy at the counter three or four people ahead of me was clearly upset with the theater employee about something. I wasn't close enough to hear exactly what he was upset about, but his voice was raised and his tone was harsh. The young woman working the stand listened patiently but was clearly embarrassed by the situation. Finally the man finished his fit and stormed past me with his large popcorn and drink. I briefly considered sticking out a foot and tripping him, but I wasn't positive that's what Jesus would do, so as he walked by I just let out a passive-aggressive laugh and shook my head at him condescendingly.*

When I reached the counter I asked the young lady, "What was that guy's problem?" She explained he was angry *because he thought she put too much popcorn in his bucket!* He didn't think he could carry it without spilling some.

*Because I think we can all agree Jesus would have at least done that.

It was then that I knew . . . Jesus *definitely* would have tripped him.

Talk about losing perspective. He looked at his bucket over-flowing with delicious, buttery popcorn and got upset because some of it was probably going to spill on the way back to his seat.

Research has proven that the more we complain, the more we find things to complain about.[1] One study separated participants into two groups. The first group was assigned to keep a daily "irritation journal" of things that annoyed them. Participants in the second group were told to keep a "thanksgiving journal" of things they were grateful for. They found those who kept thanksgiving journals had greater overall energy and enthusiasm, slept better, and were less depressed. They also discovered that what each group was assigned to do, intentionally, they started doing unintentionally. People who had to list annoyances be-came increasingly discontent. People who had to list positives became increasingly grateful. Grumbling, like grace, has a way of becoming the lens through which we look at life.

Complaining keeps us focused on what we wish was different rather than being thankful for what we have. This is why so many people who visit third-world countries come back more grateful for what they have. They've been given the gift of perspective. If you're on social media, you may have seen the hashtag #FWP. It stands for "First World Problems." Typically this is used to make fun of people who are complaining about "problems" that should be viewed as blessings. Some actual examples from the internet:

> "So frustrating to get home from the grocery store and not be able to fit the food in the fridge."
>
> "This movie is taking soooo long to download."

"I'm so sick of eating at all the restaurants near work."

"Ugh. I hate it when my Apple watch doesn't register the right distance when I run on the beach. It's clearly gonna be one of those days . . ."

Complaining causes us to become increasingly obsessed with our less-than-perfect circumstances. Gratitude, on the other hand, isn't dependent on circumstances. It recognizes that God's grace is reason enough to be thankful in all circumstances.

I know this will make me sound a little pathetic, but I sometimes struggle with contentment on airplanes. Yep, instead of appreciating the miracle of flight and being grateful that I can make a journey in a few hours that not too many years ago would have required months, I find myself discontent because I'm not in first class. I walk past first-class passengers, with their massive amounts of legroom and armrests the size of small beds, to my cramped little space in coach. I immediately put my arm on the slender armrest, because you have to stake out that territory from the beginning.* Then I grab the *Sky Mall* magazine and it ruins me. It's full of inventions you never knew existed but now realize you can't live without.† Just like the Israelites, I find myself forgetting what I have and griping about what I don't have.

God wants me to be thankful, but when I complain I lose sight of what I have to be thankful for.

A close friend of mine recently decided that instead of selling his used car or trading it in, he was going to give it to his

---

*Only one passenger is going to win!

†Don't tell my wife, but we have a robot coming in the mail. Don't worry, I got something for her too: a toilet where the lid automatically lowers after the husband walks away.

sister, who really needed it. The vehicle was worth about ten thousand dollars, it was in good shape, and he even had it serviced before signing the title over. When he gave it to his sister she said thanks, but that was about it.

A few weeks later his sister sent a text complaining about having to pay taxes on the vehicle, and a little later she complained about having to put two new tires on it. When he saw her recently, she started telling him that the air-conditioning wasn't blowing cold enough. My friend was more than annoyed by her complaining. As he finished telling me about it, here is the conclusion he reached: "I should've just traded it in. Believe me, that will be the last time I do anything like that." He was trying to be generous and thoughtful, and instead of being grateful she was constantly whining.

Complainers are going to complain. It doesn't matter how generous the provision or how thoughtful the gift, they will still find something to complain about. The more you complain the more you find something to complain about. The Israelites made up stuff to be upset about. They acted like they sat around all day in Egypt eating meat: "Hey, guys, remember when we were in Egypt we sat around the Hibachi grill and drank espressos? Those were the days."

Complaining Is Contagious

Like grace, complaining has a way of spreading. Complaining spreads from one person to another and can infect an entire community. It just takes one whiny family member, one negative neighbor, or a couple of critical church members for the community to become infected.

Complaining is contagious because the person is pointing out to everyone else how things could be better. Walk into a room and tell everyone it's too cold, and soon everyone will feel chilly. You won't notice the Thanksgiving stuffing is dry until someone points it out. It never bothered you that the game wasn't in high definition until a buddy starts talking about how much better it would be to watch the game in HD.

In Numbers 11, the grumbling started with the "riffraff," who soon had *everyone* complaining. God's people should have been positive and grateful because God had rescued them and provided for them, but instead the noise God hears from heaven is grumbling.

Reasons to Be Grateful

In his book *Seeing through the Fog,* former megachurch pastor Ed Dobson tells about his first twelve years of living with Lou Gehrig's disease, or amyotrophic lateral sclerosis (ALS). ALS is a degenerative disease with no known cause or cure. Dobson shares his ongoing struggle to give thanks while living with an incurable condition. He writes:

> There are many things for which I am not grateful. I can no longer button the buttons on my shirt. I can no longer put on a heavy jacket. I can no longer raise my right hand above my head. I can no longer write. I can no longer eat with my right hand. I eat with my left hand, and now even that is becoming a challenge. And over time all of these challenges will get worse and worse. So what in the world do I have to be grateful for?
>
> So much.
>
> Lord, thank you for waking me up this morning. Lord, thank you that I can turn over in my bed. Lord, thank you that I can still get out of bed. Lord, thank you that I can walk to the bathroom.

. . . Lord, thank you that I can still brush my teeth. . . . Lord, thank you that I can still eat breakfast. Lord, thank you that I can still dress myself. Lord, thank you that I can still drive my car. Lord, thank you that I can still walk. Lord, thank you that I can still talk. And the list goes on and on. I have learned in my journey with ALS to focus on what I can do, not on what I can't do. I have learned to be grateful for the small things in my life and for the many things I can still do.[2]

Here's a guy who is on a painful, debilitating march to death. It would seem that he has plenty to complain about, but he's not looking at life through that lens. He's looking at his circumstances through the lens of grace and he is grateful.

Complaining about Blessings?

Recently I decided to sit down and look back on my life through the lens of God's grace. What I have discovered is that I can look back on parts of my life I would have complained about to discover God's grace in them instead. I may have wished at the time things were different, but now I can see how grace has redeemed those things in my life today.

For example, I'm in my dream job because of a disgusting toilet. Let me explain. One of the greatest joys I have in my life these days is pastoring at an amazing church in Louisville, Kentucky. I know it is only by God's good grace that I have the privilege of being a part of what he is doing in this church. I'm incredibly thankful and grateful for the privilege. But what I realize now is what God used to bring me to this place often involved circumstances I complained about and situations I wished were different at the time.

Let me trace God's grace through these circumstances (I'm going to attempt to reverse engineer God's grace; stick with me on this).

Before coming to be a pastor in Louisville, I was leading a church I had started in Los Angeles County. Coming out of seminary, I didn't want to start a church; I wanted to preach. I had applied to about a dozen churches, but none of them even called me back. Apparently they weren't interested in a twenty-one-year-old preacher with no experience. I realized the only way I was going to be able to preach at a church was to start one. At the time, it didn't seem fair. I certainly wasn't thankful and thought to myself, *I wish things were different.*

The reason I wanted to be a preacher is because I fell in love with it in college. I never thought I would be a preacher. I always thought I would be a youth pastor. That was the plan. In fact, my freshman year I applied to a bunch of churches hoping to be their youth pastor, but no one was interested.

Then, one weekend, a small church in town was desperate for a preacher. They called me on a Thursday and asked me to preach that Sunday. On Sunday, I walked into a sanctuary where a couple dozen elderly people made up the congregation. Thankfully, they asked me to come back the next week, and then the next week after that, and I preached at that church for four years.

The reason I felt comfortable preaching that first weekend, even though I was only eighteen at the time, was because when I was sixteen I had a job as a tour guide at the Precious Moments Chapel in my hometown.* Yes, you can laugh.† Thousands and

*A museum of those teary-eyed figurines your grandma used to collect.
†You wouldn't laugh if you saw my collection.

thousands of guests would come to the Precious Moments Chapel every year, and I spoke to large crowds of them as their tour guide. Precious Moments has a biblical foundation, so I would get to present the gospel regularly. I never planned on working at Precious Moments. At the time, I didn't want to be working at all, and I wished things were different.

The reason I had to get a job was because not long after getting my driver's license I borrowed my mom's car to drive to Taco Hut. Taco Hut was *not* a safe place to eat. But I ate there anyway.

After eating at Taco Hut, I drove home and pulled my mom's car into the driveway and I *ran* into the house. I came out a little later and saw my mom's car in the middle of the road. It had rolled down the driveway and smashed through our mailbox. Yes, the car had significant damage. My parents told me I had to pay for the repairs. I was not thankful for those circumstances. I wished things were different, so I got a job to pay for the damages.

The reason the car rolled back down the driveway was because I forgot to put it in park. There was no way I was going to use the bathrooms at Taco Hut. They were just too sketchy.* So I sped home in a panic to get in and use the bathroom—and so neglected to put the car in park.

Are you still with me? Are you putting these pieces together? The reason I have my dream job preaching at our amazing church today is because the bathrooms in my hometown Taco Hut were disgusting!

Think about the most complaint-worthy thing in your life right now. Go ahead. Before you complain about it, consider

---

*Those bathrooms were like the Hotel California—you can go in but you might never leave.

what God's grace may be working to accomplish. What if God is going to take you through this thing and it's actually going to bring a blessing later? Ultimately our reasons for circumstantial complaining are very few because we worship a God of resurrection. If God can turn the death of Jesus into our salvation, he can do just about anything with whatever we're going through.

Not convinced? I would encourage you to try to reverse engineer God's grace in your life. You may find reasons to be grateful for God's grace at work in many of the circumstances you wish were different and a lot of what you complained about along the way.

When you got dumped by someone you really cared for, you may have wished things were different, but now that you are married to the love of your life you can look back and see God's grace.

Sometimes we look back and realize that we were complaining about a blessing.

When you didn't get accepted into that program at school, or you didn't get that promotion at work, it may not have seemed fair and you may have wished things were different, but now that you are doing what you love you can look back and see God's grace.

When you were diagnosed with cancer and going through chemotherapy, you almost certainly wished things could be different, but you saw Jesus during that time in your life and you can look back and see God's grace.

Sometimes we look back and realize that we were complaining about a blessing. God's grace was at work in our lives, but we were too busy grumbling to be grateful for it.

Forgive Me for the Days I Wasn't Grateful

I received the request from Marcus asking the church to help pay for his headstone and thought, *I have to meet this guy.* Soon, I did.

Turns out Marcus woke up one morning jaundiced. He described himself as "orange as a pumpkin." He had been a heavy drinker earlier in his life and assumed he had cirrhosis of the liver. He went to the hospital for testing—and within an hour was diagnosed with pancreatic cancer. He was told he had only a few days to live.

He was put on chemo and the progression of the cancer slowed, giving him more time than the doctors predicted.

I asked Marcus about being grateful in such difficult circumstances.

He answered, "It started . . . it started slowly. I began being grateful for the little things like clothes, my next meal, those material things, you know, that we consider our daily bread. And I began to see things through . . . through different eyes. Now I see things in an eternal light: how this life will have a profound effect on my next life, and how anticipation of the next life is having a profound effect on this life I have now. And it's been truly amazing."

I asked about the inscription he wanted on his headstone.

He said, "I want to forward a message on to any wayward passerby who comes across my headstone and maybe identifies with it, and who has the eyes to discern the message. And the simple line is: forgive me for the days I was not grateful. And in that one sentence it states my problem: I was not grateful. And it also includes the solution: forgive me. And that's the message that I want to pass on."

Message received.

God, forgive us for the days we were not grateful.

Give us the grace to recognize your grace and to know that your grace is always reason enough to be thankful, even when we wish things were different.

More Powerful
Than Your Weakness

I recently learned about an artist named Phil Hansen. He's a huge success. His breakthrough approach to creating art has made him incredibly popular and has inspired millions of people. I became familiar with Hansen's art by watching his TED talk called "Embrace the Shake." If you haven't seen it, I encourage you to pull it up and take ten minutes to watch it.

In art school Phil began to develop a tremor in his hand. For years he had worked toward becoming an expert in pointillism, a technique where the artist uses small, distinct dots to form an image. Years of tediously making tiny dots had led to permanent nerve damage, making it impossible for him to hold his hand steady. Suddenly Phil's signature ability—making beautiful images out of small, perfect dots—became his signature disability. His strength had become his weakness. He quit art for a while, but his neurologist said something that stuck with him.

"Why don't you just embrace the shake?"

Finally Phil started experimenting with art again, and the most incredible thing happened. The shake that he thought had destroyed his artistic ability became what inspired his most powerful work. His weakness became his strength.

Phil realized that what he thought were his limitations became a catalyst for greater creativity. He became convinced of this dynamic and wondered what kind of art he could produce if he intentionally put limitations on himself. What if he could use only a dollar's worth of supplies? What if he had to paint but couldn't use a brush? What if he made art not to display but to destroy? What if he had to rely on other people to come up with his content? He learned to "embrace the shake" and discovered that art created out of weakness ended up being his most inspiring pieces. He explains it this way: "We need to first be limited in order to become limitless."[1]

Refusing Weakness

It's not easy to "embrace the shake." We have grown up learning we need to highlight our strengths and hide our weaknesses. We don't embrace our limitations; we're embarrassed by them, so much so we often refuse to admit them.

We sometimes watch *Shark Tank* at our house, a show in which inventors and entrepreneurs seek financial partners by pitching their products or businesses to a group of five wealthy venture capitalists. More often than not, when I'm listening to one of the inventors tell about their new product, I wonder, *Why didn't I think of that?* And I can't be the only one who has watched the show and thought, *Wait a second, I did think of that!*

If you watch the show you may remember an invention called "The Skinny Mirror." This mirror uses curved glass to create an optical illusion so the user will look about ten pounds thinner. It was originally designed for individuals, but its creators found that retailers were very interested in using the mirror to help sell clothing. If you are trying on clothes at the store and you use "The Skinny Mirror" to see how they fit, you're much more likely to make a purchase. What I found especially interesting about "The Skinny Mirror" is that they don't try to hide what it is. In fact, they put their name right on the mirror. So the next time you're at a store trying on a pair of skinny jeans and love what you see in the mirror, whatever you do, don't look at the bottom right-hand corner for "The Skinny Mirror" logo. You might be devastated.

I was thinking someone could probably develop an entire product line around the idea that we don't want to admit the truth about our weakness. Here are a few ideas I had:

1. "The Skinny Scale," a complementary product to "The Skinny Mirror." When you weigh yourself on this scale, it gives you a number ten pounds lighter than reality. That way what you see on the scale matches up with what you see in the mirror!

2. "The Skinny Bowl." Want to eat an entire pint of Ben & Jerry's but don't want to feel guilty about it? Just put it in "The Skinny Bowl." Don't worry, this doesn't mean you'll get any less. "The Skinny Bowl" would be a *huge* bowl designed as an optical illusion to make you feel like you're eating less than you really are.

3. "Skinny Glasses." You realize your mirror makes you look great, and your scale is backing it up, but what will your

blind date actually see? Just ask them to put on a pair of "Skinny Glasses," and they'll see exactly what you want them to see!

Denying weakness can be a lucrative business!

Beautiful Circle

We would much prefer a magic mirror that lies to us rather than one that tells us the truth about ourselves. But we all experience moments when we are confronted with the truth of our limitations.

I came home from work one day with no clue that anything was wrong. My wife greeted me at the door and told me that Morgan, our two-year-old daughter, was still napping but had been sleeping long enough, and asked me to go wake her up. That's a job I loved.* When I opened the door to her room I noticed that a large pine chest of drawers had fallen over onto the floor. Initially, the possibility that Morgan was under the chest of drawers didn't occur to me. I looked around the room for her and called her name—before I realized she had to be under there.

I frantically lifted the piece of furniture. Morgan looked life-less . . . not moving or making any kind of noise. I yelled for my wife. Morgan was breathing but she was unconscious. She was black-and-blue and so swollen that she didn't look like herself. I grabbed the phone and dialed 911—it rang and rang—but no one answered. I hung up. My wife had Morgan in her arms as we ran out to the car to rush to the hospital.

*She's sixteen now, so waking her up . . . not as much fun.

I was driving and my wife was in the backseat holding our daughter. I called 911 again, but still got no answer. It rang and rang. I was scared and was getting angry. The first time in my life I ever call 911 and no one picks up! I felt so powerless. Desperate. There was nothing I could do to help.

I was getting ready to dial 911 again, and if someone didn't answer this time, 911 was going to have to dial 911 by the time I got finished with them. But then I could hear my wife praying over Morgan, crying out to God from the backseat. I hung up and started praying out loud with her. Our prayers were not orderly, and they were not well worded. I didn't say to my wife, "You pray, then I'll pray." They sounded more like cries than a conversation.

Eventually we got to the hospital and ran in. Morgan still wasn't moving or making any noise. The next few minutes are a bit of a blur for me. Doctors and nurses surrounded her as they decided what tests they needed to run to find out what was wrong. They looked for internal bleeding, skull fractures, broken bones. They were able to help Morgan regain consciousness and wake up—but she still wasn't responding to us. They took her in to do X-rays and an MRI. They would only let one parent go back in the room with her. My wife went straight in, and I was left out in the hallway by myself.*

I slumped down, sat against the wall, and continued to pray and cry out to God. If people were around, I don't remember, and it wouldn't have mattered. I didn't care what anyone thought. I wasn't worried about what I looked like or how I sounded. Desperate people don't care about such things.

*Now that I think about it, the decision as to which parent should go in wasn't handled very diplomatically. There was no discussion. We didn't take a vote.

We spent the evening at the hospital. The doctors told us there didn't seem to be any internal damage, but for some reason Morgan wasn't able to move her left leg. The doctor explained there was a lot the medical community didn't yet know about nerve damage . . . he didn't think it was permanent but had no way of knowing when she would be able to move her leg.

Weeks later she still couldn't move her leg, and we were warned the muscles in her legs might begin to atrophy. But what could I do? I couldn't do anything. Every morning my wife and I would go into her room and wake her up and pray for her. And every morning we'd say the same thing: "Morgan, move your toes." "Wiggle your toes, Morgan." And every day she would look at her toes with a very determined stare. After a few moments she would look up at us with a smile and say, "They don't work."

But then one day . . . they did. They only moved a little, but they moved. Eventually all of the nerve damage was healed. Morgan made a full recovery and was back to running around.

Looking back, sitting on the cold floor of that hospital hallway, I remember the feeling of utter helplessness. There was nothing I could do. Here's the thing, though: God had never felt closer or more real to me than he did in that moment. I have prayed in beautiful sanctuaries and I've worshiped in packed arenas, but God showed up most powerfully to me in a cold, lonely, quiet hospital hallway. My complete powerlessness was a necessary precondition to experiencing God's total power and presence.

Perhaps you've been in a place where you could not deny you didn't have what it takes.

If not, it's coming.

If you have, it was probably a painful experience for you. But the truth about that moment is, while it may have been full of pain, it also had the most potential to be full of God's power. Why? Because we're able to receive God's grace only to the extent we're able to recognize our need for it.

We live in a culture that celebrates strength and condemns weakness, but grace enables us to celebrate our weakness. When we celebrate our weakness, it opens the floodgates for grace to pour into our lives. When grace pours into our lives, it allows us to celebrate our weakness all the more.

We're able to receive God's grace only to the extent we're able to recognize our need for it.

It's a circle, a beautiful circle.

If God's power works best in weakness, then recognizing *I don't have what it takes* will enable you to receive God's grace, which enables you to celebrate your weakness, which makes room for more grace to pour into your life. You get caught up in a beautiful circle of grace.

Power in Weakness

The more we are able to acknowledge our weakness, the greater our opportunity to experience God's power in our lives. This doesn't come naturally to me. More often than not I'm the last person who is able to identify my weakness.

I went to Walmart recently to buy ink for my home printer. While I was there I saw a rack of shorts on sale for only $10. I thought, *It's almost summer. I could use shorts. And only ten bucks!* so I grabbed a pair of 34s. I didn't try them on because . . . I'm a guy. That's not what we do. The next day I went to put on the shorts, but they were too tight. I mean, I was able to get them buttoned. But the button was scared; it was hanging on for dear life!

Guess what I *never* thought? I never thought, *I might have put on a few pounds.* Why not? Because that would be admitting weakness, and if I'm being honest I prefer not to do that. So the first thought that came to my mind was, *You get what you pay for.* The second: *Walmart must have marked them down to ten dollars because they didn't measure the size correctly. These shorts must actually be a 30-inch waist.*

I can laugh about this when it's about a pair of tight-fitting shorts that cost me ten bucks, but my refusal to be honest with myself about my struggles and weakness has been much more costly to me as a husband, father, friend, and pastor.

When I can identify the areas where I don't have what it takes and be intentional about asking God for help, his grace and power abound.

The Thorny Ache

Paul learned to not only acknowledge his weakness but celebrate it. In the Bible we have two letters Paul wrote to the church in Corinth. Corinth was a city that celebrated strength. It was known for luxurious lifestyles, impressive architecture, and elite socialites. A destination city, Corinth was the place to go for pleasure and exotic living. And the Corinthian style of architecture was characterized by massive columns with amazing detail that were constructed to portray power.

After Paul wrote his first letter to the Corinthians, some false teachers came into the city and began winning people over with their boasting. They held up their religious résumés and bragged about their amazing spiritual experiences.

Paul wants the Corinthians to see how wrong these false teachers are. He wants the Corinthians to learn to celebrate their weaknesses. But Paul knows the only way they'll listen to him talk about weakness is if they know his strengths, so he has to start there. He feels a little foolish talking about his qualifications and credentials, but he knows that it's the only way they'll listen to him when he talks about the value of being weak. And so he begins:

> Whatever anyone else dares to boast about—I am speaking as a fool—I also dare to boast about. Are they Hebrews? So am I. Are they Israelites? So am I. Are they Abraham's descendants? So am I. Are they servants of Christ? (I am out of my mind to talk like this.) (2 Cor. 11:21–23)

Then he goes on to explain how his strengths and experiences could have led him to put confidence in himself, to think *I have what it takes*. But watch how he continues:

> So to keep me from becoming proud, I was given a thorn in my flesh, a messenger from Satan to torment me and keep me from becoming proud. Three different times I begged the Lord to take it away. (12:7–8 NLT)

What was Paul's "thorn in the flesh"? Bible scholars have suggested many possibilities, but no one is sure. We'll take a look at some possibilities, but I wonder if Paul leaves it vague in order to make it easier for us to fill in the blank with our own thorn.

What's yours? What have you begged God to change, to heal, to take away? What in your life forces you to acknowledge weakness?

My weakness is: _____.

160   Grace Is Greater . . . Than Your Circumstances

What would you write in that blank? Again, the idea of this book is not that you *learn* grace is greater than your weakness but that you *experience* God's grace by receiving his power in your weakness. Keep your weakness in mind as we consider what it might have been for Paul.

Paul's Thorn

I've thought about what Paul might have written in that blank. He could have written the word *infirmities*. The Bible hints Paul may not have been the best-looking guy. Other verses indicate he may have had terrible vision or even epilepsy. If it was a physical infirmity Paul is referring to, he discovered God's grace was greater.

Joni Eareckson Tada learned a similar lesson. As a teenager she became a quadriplegic through a diving accident. She has since become a popular Christian writer, and in one article she tells this story:

> Honesty is always the best policy, but especially when you're surrounded by a crowd of women in a restroom during a break at a Christian women's conference. One woman, putting on lipstick, said, "Oh, Joni, you always look so together, so happy in your wheelchair. I wish that I had your joy!" Several women around her nodded. "How do you do it?" she asked as she capped her lipstick.
>
> "I don't do it," I said. "In fact, may I tell you honestly how I woke up this morning?
>
> "This is an average day." I breathed deeply. "After my husband, Ken, leaves for work at 6:00 a.m., I'm alone until I hear the front door open at 7:00 a.m. That's when a friend arrives to get me up.

"While I listen to her make coffee, I pray, 'Oh, Lord, my friend will soon give me a bath, get me dressed, sit me up in my chair, brush my hair and teeth, and send me out the door. I don't have the strength to face this routine one more time. I have no resources. I don't have a smile to take into the day. But you do. May I have yours? God, I need you desperately.'"

"So, what happens when your friend comes through the bedroom door?" one of them asked.

"I turn my head toward her and give her a smile sent straight from heaven. It's not mine. It's God's. And so," I said, gesturing to my paralyzed legs, "whatever joy you see today was hard won this morning."

I have learned that the weaker we are, the more we need to lean on God; and the more we lean on God, the stronger we discover him to be.[2]

I wonder if you have some infirmities you've begged God to take away, but he hasn't. And I wonder if they've forced you to lean on God.

Another word Paul could have written in that blank is *inabilities*. We don't know if this was his "thorn," but several times Paul mentions he was not an eloquent or persuasive speaker. In this case God's grace came crashing into Paul's life in such a powerful way that for years he was the primary spokesperson for Christianity. He wrote about half of the New Testament. When we are weak, God is strong.

I think of my somewhat introverted nature. Being around too many people for too long can be draining for me. I wish it wasn't. It's something I struggle with. To be honest, I struggle with the fact that it's a struggle for me. I believe God has called me to be a pastor, and the thing about being a pastor is it often means being around a lot of people. I work with some pastors who are fantastic in those settings and are energized by other people. I've envied them and asked God to help me become more extroverted. He hasn't. I've learned the only way I can "have what it takes" to be a pastor is to lean into God and be intentional about finding my strength in him. I've also come to realize God's power in my weakness by using it in some unexpected and surprising ways.

What inability torments you? Perhaps it's something about you that you wish was different, but maybe that's the very area where God's power will use you most significantly.

One other word Paul could write in that blank is *inadequacy*. Paul at times expresses feelings of inadequacy. He found himself in situations where he couldn't help but come to the conclusion, "I don't have what it takes." He talks about the challenges he has gone through in his ministry and his feelings of inadequacy in the calling God gave him.

God's power is attracted to weakness. His grace comes running to those in need.

In 2 Corinthians 1:8 Paul explains, "We were under great pressure, far beyond our ability to endure." Paul realizes the weight on the bar is more than he can lift. He is humble enough to be honest with himself and admit his abilities are not equal to his assignment. So why would God allow this kind of mismatch to happen?

In verse 9 Paul gives us the answer to this question: "This happened that we might not rely on ourselves but on God, who raises the dead." God's power is attracted to weakness. His grace comes running to those in need.

Whatever you filled in the blank with, whatever your thorn is, his grace is greater than that.

Celebrating Weakness

We aren't exactly sure what word Paul would use to fill in the blank for his weakness. But he makes it clear God's grace is always enough.

> Each time he said, "My grace is all you need. My power works best in weakness." So now I am glad to boast about my weaknesses, so that the power of Christ can work through me. That's why I take pleasure in my weaknesses, and in the insults, hardships, persecutions, and troubles that I suffer for Christ. For when I am weak, then I am strong. (12:9–10 NLT)

A lot of people have memorized that verse as "My grace is sufficient." Another translation says, "My grace is always enough." We're then told that his strength is perfected in weakness. That is, it fills in our blanks. The wider the blank, the more of his grace and strength can be displayed.

Grace enabled Paul to celebrate his weakness. Celebrating his weakness opened the floodgate for more grace to pour into his life, which further allowed him to celebrate his weakness.

Paul's thorn helped him realize he was able to receive God's grace only to the extent he was able to recognize his need for it. Paul's experience of that truth led him to "take pleasure in his weakness." He became more excited about his weakness than his power, because in his weakness there was room for God to show up and show off what he could do. Acknowledging weakness invites God's presence and power into our lives.

Source of Strength

The latest way I have recognized how our culture celebrates strength is in a growing trend of giving job titles that overstate the importance of a position. In the big scheme of things, some-one using an exaggerated job title isn't a huge deal, but there are times when it crosses the line. Here are some examples I've collected:

- An ad for a "Retail Salesperson" offered the position as a "Retail Jedi."
- A "Marketing Manager" handed me a business card with the title "Marketing Rock Star."
- Instead of the title of "Social Media Manager," a friend of mine was hired to be a "Social Media Guru."
- Go online and you will find there are a number of "Financial Managers" who have opted to go with the title "Accounting Ninja."*

I understand the appeal of using job titles like these, but it doesn't quite seem fair to all the hardworking Jedi, rock stars, gurus, and ninjas out there. I get it, though. Part of me would love to be a "Preaching Jedi" or "Leadership Wizard" or "Servant Rock Star."

We love strength. I'm not sure that's likely to change, so the questions I'd pose are:

- Where do you find strength?
- How much strength do you want?

Maybe you can find it in your own store of willpower, but you probably have lived long enough to realize there's not much strength available to you there. God wants you to find strength in him—unlimited strength.

*Deadly but boring assassins. Weapon of choice: spreadsheets.

We see this all through the Bible. Moses, Gideon, Elijah, the apostles, Paul—all were intimidated by their calling. But God gave each of them the same reassurance. "I will be with you," God says. "It's fine that you don't have what it takes, because I *do* have what it takes, and I will be with you." By the grace of God, his strength works best in our weakness.

Let It Flow

Close your eyes and imagine something. OK, that's not going to work, because you can't read with your eyes shut, but try to imagine this.

In your hand is a simple cup. It's empty, and the emptiness represents your weakness. But someone directs you to a nearby hose. It's coming out of a very high and very long wall. You can't see the other side, but the faucet works. You turn it on and water begins to seep from the hose. It's not spraying—just kind of trickling. You're hoping there's enough to at least fill your cup. The water moves right up to the rim, then stops. That worked out well.

You get the symbolism? Right—the water represents God's grace, exactly what we need. (I always worry people won't get my metaphors.)

Time passes, and here you come, back to the hose. No sign of the cup, but you've got an empty bucket this time. Let's make the bucket a symbol of having a bit of a health scare, or maybe some financial issues. You really need some strength; this is a nice-sized bucket.

You turn on the hose and the water comes again, gradually filling in the bottom of the bucket, then up the sides, and once again to the rim before it stops. *How does it know?*

Time passes. This time you have a large, red wheelbarrow full of emptiness, and you've brought it to the old hose. Maybe you've lost your job, and with it your confidence. Or maybe your marriage is in a bad place, worse than you realized. Maybe it's a special-needs child and you're overwhelmed.

You turn on the hose and the plumbing still works. The water comes out with that familiar *swish*, and the wheelbarrow begins to fill. And you know where it stops. You sigh with relief. Once again, there's just enough.

The emptier we are, the more of his grace we can receive. The weaker we are, the more of his strength we can discover.

Next time you pull up in a semitruck, hauling a tank behind you the size of a trailer. This is big. Radiation treatments. A child in prison. An affair. You turn on the hose. Water begins to flow into the tank. You're sure there won't be enough, but it keeps coming. For hours it flows—and then right when the tank won't take another drop, the hose runs dry.

This is how the grace of God works. There is always enough. However much emptiness you bring to him, that is how much grace he has to give you. The emptier we are, the more of his grace we can receive. The weaker we are, the more of his strength we can discover. That's why Paul says he can take pleasure in his weakness.

Time to Give Up

A number of years ago I was with my family on a road trip. We had spent hours traveling and pulled into a hotel parking lot around 2:00 a.m. I woke up my wife and kids, and in a zombie state we made our way into the hotel. My son was four years old and had insisted on carrying his own bag throughout the trip. He was at that age where he wanted to impress us with his strength. He would randomly flex his muscles to show them off or pick up something heavy just so he could show us he could do it. So even though he was half asleep, he picked up his bag from the trunk, slung the strap over his shoulder, and began to stagger his way slowly across the parking lot.

I was carrying a few bags and following behind when he suddenly stopped in the middle of the parking lot and let his bag fall off his shoulder and onto the pavement. I walked beside him and stopped. His eyes were barely open. I said, "Hey buddy, do you want me to carry your bag for you?" Too tired to verbally respond, he nodded his head yes. I picked up his bag and threw it over my shoulder and started toward the hotel door. After a few strides I looked back at my son and realized he wasn't moving. I turned around and walked back to him. His shoulders were slumped and his head was down. He was exhausted. I asked him if he was OK, and without even looking up at me he asked, "Will you carry me too, Dad?" I scooped him up in my arms and headed into the hotel.

I know he wanted to show us how strong he was, but he reached a point where he was too tired and felt too weak to keep going. As a father, I wasn't disappointed or angry with him. In fact, it brought me joy to be able to help him in the moment. He didn't feel like he could go any farther. He didn't have to drop the bag and ask for help. He could have insisted on carrying it himself. But the longer he refused to admit his weakness, the longer he missed out on the strength available to help him. The moment he dropped what he was carrying he discovered a grace that didn't just carry his bag but carried him as well.

You're never in a better position to experience God's grace than the moment you realize you don't have what it takes.

10

More Hopeful
Than Your Despair

In 1921 a missionary couple from Sweden named David and Svea Flood went with their two-year-old son to the heart of Africa, to what was then called the Belgian Congo. They met up with another missionary couple and the four of them decided to take the gospel to a remote area where people had never heard about Jesus.

Unfortunately, when they arrived, the chief of the tribe wouldn't let them live in the village. They were forced to live about a mile away, and their only contact with anyone from the village was with a young boy whom the chief allowed to come sell them food. Svea ended up leading that young boy to faith in Jesus, but that was their *only* progress. They never had contact with anyone else from the village. Eventually the other couple contracted malaria and left. The Floods were on their own. And soon Svea, who was pregnant, also contracted malaria. She died several days after giving birth.

Her husband dug a crude grave, buried his twenty-seven-year-old wife, and went back to the main mission station. He gave his newborn baby girl to the missionaries there and said, "I'm going back to Sweden. I've lost my wife. I obviously can't take care of this baby. God has ruined my life." And he took his son and left. Missionaries adopted his baby daughter and brought her back to the United States to raise her.

At this point in the story I can't help but wonder why a man of such faith would respond this way. I have never had to deal with this kind of disappointment and heartache, but it seems like the pain was just too much. His life seemed completely ruined. Beyond repair. From his perspective this was how his story ended. There was no coming back from such loss.

The End or the Middle?

When I was young, there was a series of kids' books that was quite popular called Choose Your Own Adventure. Each story allowed the reader at different points in the story to choose between several different endings. So if you wanted the story to go one direction, you turned to page 73, but if you wanted it to go a different direction you turned to page 96. If you started reading the option on page 73 and didn't like how the plot was unfolding, then you simply stopped reading and tried an alternate ending.

These Choose Your Own Adventure books have sold more than 250 million copies over the years. I'm not surprised at their popularity, because most of us would prefer a story we can control. We like the idea that we can change our circumstances and decide our own outcomes. It would be nice if life had an Option B that would allow us to avoid adversity and dodge difficulties.

Eventually we all reach a point in our story where we don't want to keep reading. The challenge is too overwhelming. The relationship is too broken. The situation is too impossible. The pain is too much. I think David Flood had reached that point.

What if what feels like the end of the story is actually just the middle?

Have you ever reached a point like that? You deal with as much as you can for as long as you can, but eventually the pain becomes too much. Here's my question: What if what feels like the end of the story is actually just the middle?

When God is the author of your story, you can trust that his grace will have the final word. God's grace can redeem anything. One of the most beautiful verses about the power of God's grace is Romans 8:28:

> And we know that in all things God works for the good of those who love him, who have been called according to his purpose.

Paul tells us that the author of our stories, the one directing our lives, *is* trustworthy and *is* going to bring a good ending no matter how bad the chapter we're currently reading might seem. That's the promise of grace. But let's be honest:

when you're the one who's hurting,
when it's your health that's failing,
when it's your marriage that's falling apart,
when it's your child who is struggling,

when it's your job that has been eliminated, and

when the pain is too much,

the idea that God's grace can work things out for the good seems at best naïve but more likely offensive. When the pain seems too much, simple platitudes don't do much to make us feel better.

This promise must have seemed just as unbelievable to the Christians in Rome who first received it. Because of their faith, they faced potential loss of their jobs, family relationships, and even their lives.

Paul recognizes some of the difficulties they were facing when he mentions hardships, persecution, famine, nakedness, danger, and the sword. He assures them that "in all these things we are more than conquerors through him who loved us" (v. 37) and that nothing "will be able to separate us from the love of God that is in Christ Jesus our Lord" (v. 39). Paul wants these Christians to understand that no matter how desperate things may seem in the moment, God's love and grace will win the day.

He wasn't calling for blind optimism. He doesn't say, "And we think that in all things God will work for the good." He doesn't say, "And we believe/hope/are pretty sure . . ." He says, "*We know* God works for the good of those who love him."

I dug into the Greek word that is translated "we know" and discovered it means an absolute, unshakable confidence. Paul is speaking with the certainty of a man who has glimpsed the redeeming work of God's grace in his life.

This word translated "we know" is used one other time in Romans 8. In verse 22, Paul is talking about the pain of this life and how this world can be a pretty messed-up place. He writes, "*We know* that the whole creation has been groaning."

In other words, Paul says two things are absolutely sure:

1. Life is hard (v. 22).
2. God is good (v. 28).

Paul is unshakably confident about these two truths. But sometimes the space between them feels like an eternity.

Just Keep Reading

My middle daughter loves to read. When she reads a novel she enters into the story and emotionally engages with the characters. When she was younger it wasn't unusual for her to become stressed out about halfway through the book and stop reading it. I found myself encouraging her with three words that maybe you need to hear at this point in your story: "Just keep reading."

The story isn't over yet. The final chapter has yet to be written. Trust the Author. If you're in the middle of a chapter titled "Life Is Hard," you can know for certain that you will soon come to a chapter titled "God Is Good." Just keep reading.

All this reminds me of the 2014 Winter Olympics, which were in China, so the events took place while most Americans were sleeping. I tried to avoid finding out who won each competition before it aired on TV, but it was difficult. One night my family was watching couples ice dancing.* I had read earlier that Americans Meryl Davis and Charlie White had won the first gold medal ever for the United States in this event. But my family had no idea I already knew who won.

As the Americans performed their ice dancing routine, I expressed my confidence that *this* was a gold medal performance.

*I am not a proud man.

I tried to impress my daughters with my understanding of the intricacies of ice dancing. When it was announced that Davis and White had won the gold, I couldn't tell if my kids were proud or embarrassed that their dad was such an expert in ice dancing.

I have to admit: it was kind of fun knowing the ending before the ending.

And it's not just me. Two UC San Diego researchers conducted a study that suggested spoilers don't actually spoil stories. They ran three experiments using twelve stories. They discovered people consistently enjoyed the story *more* if the ending had been spoiled than if they read the story in suspense. One of the researchers had an interesting theory about why people like to know the end of the story before the ending. He said, "So it could be that once you know how it turns out, it's cognitively easier—you're more comfortable processing the information—and can focus on a deeper understanding of the story."[1] Maybe he's right. When a story has been spoiled, it's easier to follow and understand. We lose some of the suspense, but perhaps knowing how it will end allows us to not just endure the journey but actually enjoy it.

Paul doesn't give a spoiler alert but he does tell us how the story ends. Because of grace, we know that in all things God works for the good of those who love him and are called according to his purpose.

Sometimes you just have to keep reading.

David Flood's Story

Let me finish telling you about David Flood, the Swedish missionary who moved his young family all the way to Africa to see just one child come to faith. Then he lost his wife to malaria soon after she gave birth to their daughter. Furious with God, David buried his wife, gave his baby away to a missionary couple from the United States, and went back to Sweden with his small son.

Well, that daughter was given the name Aggie and grew up in the United States with Christian parents. One day she checked her mailbox and for some unknown reason found a Swedish magazine. She was flipping through it when a photo stopped her cold. It was a picture of a crude grave with a white cross. On the cross was the name "Svea Flood." She recognized her mother's name. She took the magazine to someone who could translate the story that accompanied the photo. Aggie sat and listened to the story about the work her mother had done as a missionary.

Sometime later she traveled to Sweden to find her father. Turns out he had remarried, fathered four more children, and basically ruined his life with alcohol.

After an emotional meeting with her half siblings, Aggie brought up the subject of seeing her father. They hesitated and then explained, "You can talk to him, but he's very ill. And you need to know that whenever he hears the name of God, he flies into a rage."

Aggie wasn't deterred. She walked into his tiny apartment, saw empty liquor bottles everywhere, and approached the seventy-three-year-old man who had deserted her years before.

As soon as she said "Papa?" he began to cry and apologized profusely. She smiled. "It's all right, Papa. God took care of me." Instantly he stiffened and his tears stopped. "God forgot all of us," he said, turning his face to the wall. "Our lives have been like this because of him."

"Papa," Aggie said, "I've got a story to tell you, and it's a true one. The little boy you and Mama led to the Lord grew up to lead his entire village to faith in Jesus. The one seed you planted just kept growing and growing. Today more than six hundred African people are serving the Lord because you were faithful to the call of God in your life. You didn't go to Africa in vain. Mama didn't die in vain. Papa, Jesus loves you. He has never hated you."[2]

David was stunned. His muscles relaxed, and their conversation continued. By the end of the day he had come back to the God he had resented for so many decades, and within weeks he walked through the doorway of death and into his eternal home with God in heaven.

I'm thankful for what God did as David Flood lived out his last weeks on earth. But I can't help but think that David could have handled his pain so much better if he just hadn't lost faith in God's goodness. If only he would have believed that God's grace is greater. What if, instead of closing the book, he would have just kept reading?

God's Definition of Good

One of the reasons we have a hard time believing that God's grace is working for good in our lives is because of how we define the word *good*. We have our own ideas of how God should work for our good, ideas that range from a cancer-free report to an on-time flight.

A few years ago I realized that my driver's license had expired. (I realized this when the cop explained it to me.) I went to the DMV to get a new driver's license and was told that since mine had been expired for so long, I would have to take the test all over again. Spending the afternoon at the DMV taking a driver's test with a room full of sixteen-year-olds was not how I planned to spend the day, but I wasn't worried. I had been driving for over a decade and was sure I would breeze through the test.

But as I started taking the test, I quickly realized I was in trouble. Then I took it up to the officer and she started grading it right in front of me. She had her red pen out, and I started keeping track of how many I'd missed. It reached a point when I realized if I missed one more, I was going to fail. Not an acceptable outcome. I imagined calling my wife from the DMV and saying, "Could you come pick me up? I failed my driver's test." It would be a confirmation of everything she'd ever said about my driving, and I would never hear the end of it. As the officer finished grading my test, I began praying, *Jesus, if you're really listening . . .*

She got down to the last question, looked up at me with a slight smile, and said, "Did you mean to mark the letter B on this answer?" And I suddenly sensed God working in my life. The DMV office is not a place he usually frequents, but he showed up that day.

I looked at the question, but I still wasn't sure what the right answer was. So I started stalling. "Did I put the letter B? That's not what I meant to put . . ."

She could see I was struggling. "Did you mean to mark the letter C?"

"I was going to say C right before you said C," I said. "That's what I was going to say." She marked out B, circled C, and in all things God works for the good.

I tend to think that if God is working for my good, then everything that happens to me should work out according to my definition of good, like my day at the DMV. But when something not so good happens to me, it doesn't seem like God is keeping his promise. We tend to think God working for our good means we won't experience pain and will somehow be exempt from the suffering of this world. But God's definition of good is different from that.

The Goodness of Grace

So what is God's definition of good? Let me give you a few ways you can know that God's grace is at work in the midst of your pain to bring about goodness in your life.

1. You can know God's grace is working in your pain to draw you closer to Jesus.

God doesn't waste our pain but rather can use it and work in it to call our hearts closer to him. Here's how The Living Bible paraphrases 2 Corinthians 7:10: "For God sometimes uses sorrow in our lives to help us turn away from sin and seek eternal life."

My guess is that this is exactly what happens for many of you. You go through something incredibly difficult, and in the midst of it you discover Jesus in a way that you have never known him before. What you thought was the worst thing that ever happened to you ended up being the best thing that ever happened to you because it brought you closer to Jesus.

That's the difference grace makes. It doesn't always take away our pain but it does something better—it redeems it. In our pain, we discover the presence of Jesus in a way that we never would have otherwise.

2. You can know that God's grace is working in your pain to make you more like Jesus.

God's grace takes all the broken pieces of our lives and puts them together so that we look more like Jesus. After promising us that in all things God is working for the good in our lives, Paul gives us a further explanation of at least one way God brings about goodness. Romans 8:29 reads, "For those God foreknew he also predestined to be conformed to the image of his Son."

Paul speaks of those God "foreknew." God is all-knowing and his knowledge isn't limited to a linear timeline. He lives outside of time and space and sees everything at once. He not only knows everything that has happened but also everything that will happen as if it already has happened. You'll never hear God say, "Wow, I didn't see that coming." And in his foreknowledge, he knows everything, good or bad, pleasurable or painful, that will ever happen to you.

Then we are told what God has done with that knowledge: he has predestined—that is, predetermined—that all things in life will work for our good by conforming us to the image of Christ. Knowing what you would go through, God made a decision ahead of time to use all of that to make you more like Jesus. That means your pain always has a purpose. There's a big difference between pain that has a purpose and pain that seems pointless.

Pain with Purpose

A number of years ago, when I was young and foolish, I got into a discussion with my wife about the pain of childbirth. She was fairly convinced that if men had to endure the level of pain that accompanies giving birth, the world would have never been populated. I did a little research and discovered that the closest pain comparison that men endure is passing kidney stones. From a purely physical perspective, having kidney stones and giving birth are two events that are fairly close on the pain chart.

Knowing that men pass kidney stones quite often, I thought it best to bring this evidence to my wife so that she could have the appropriate level of appreciation for the pain tolerance of the male half of the species.

She considered the evidence, pointed out that the study was done by a man who had never been in labor for ten-plus hours and had never given birth. But then she made a great point. "There is a big difference in choosing pain versus having no choice." Meaning that women are tougher because they consciously choose to endure pain, whereas no man has ever chosen to pass a kidney stone. "I'm excited to pass a kidney stone," said no man ever.

I didn't admit it to my wife, but I thought she made a great point. Choosing to go through pain is a different level of toughness than being forced to go through pain. The question is: Why would a woman choose to go through pain? It's because she knows that *the pain has a purpose*.

She is willing to endure the pain because she is more focused on what the pain will produce. In fact, after going through the excruciating pain of childbirth, a woman might say, "That was so rewarding. I hope God blesses me with another pregnancy." But no man who has ever passed a kidney stone would say anything like that.

The difference in the pain of childbirth and the pain of kidney stones is that the pain of childbirth produces something good and precious. There is a purpose that comes from the pain. As long as we can have confidence that pain has a purpose, we can find the strength to endure.

Paul reminds us it is God's grace that gives us this confidence. His grace in our pain is a promise that whatever pain we go through in this life does not get wasted. It will give birth to something good.

As a pastor, I have had hundreds of people come to me looking for answers when their pain seems too much. One of the comments I often hear goes something like this: "Everything happens for a *reason*. I know God has a *reason* for this." When the pain of life is overwhelming, we are desperate to make sense of it. We think if there is a reason behind it, the pain won't hurt as much. But I'm not sure there is always a reason, and even if there is one, I'm quite sure we won't always understand it.

Here's how I've tried to encourage people to reframe that question. Instead of asking "What is the reason?" we should ask "What is the *purpose*?" Because I don't know if there is always a reason, but I know God in his grace always has a purpose.

What's the difference between "reason" and "purpose"? Reason looks for a *because*, but purpose focuses on the *for*. Reason wants a logical explanation that will make sense out of something that has happened. Purpose offers us a hope that whatever has happened God can work for good.

Do you remember what Jesus said when he and his disciples came across a man who had been born blind (John 9), or when he got the news that a tower had fallen over in Siloam and killed eighteen innocent people (Luke 13)? People came and asked him, "Why has this happened? What's the explanation?" The people wanted a reason. But Jesus told them they were asking the wrong question. He explained, in so many words, "These things happen, but watch for the work of God to be accomplished here." Jesus didn't give them a reason but he assured them there was a purpose.

God's grace to us in our pain is that our pain is not without purpose. God can work through it to make us more like Jesus.

When Grace Hurts

Harold Wilke was born with no arms, and as he grew up many tasks that came naturally to other kids were extraordinarily difficult for him. He tells of a time, as a very young child, when he was on the floor struggling to put his shirt on. His mom and her neighbor friend stood and watched as he writhed around on the floor. The neighbor said to his mom, "Why don't you help that poor child?" His mom stood with her arms held stiffly at her sides and her jaw clamped tight as she resisted every instinct and finally, through gritted teeth, responded, "I am helping him."

I know when you're going through suffering or you're living with pain it may seem that God, who is all-powerful, should do something to help. Consider the possibility that God in his grace *is* helping. Sometimes grace hurts so that it can help. It's hard to find grace in cancer, but maybe God allows the cancer to help us take stock of our lives and help us and those around us think about eternity. It's hard to find God's grace when you can't stand your boss, but maybe God allows a difficult boss to help us learn to be self-controlled and not find our identity in a job. It's hard to find grace in unemployment, but maybe he allows unemployment to help us understand that we are dependent on him. Maybe he allows the pain of a broken heart to expose our idolatry and help us learn to put our hope in him. The list could go on and on. How has this been true in your life? God's grace to you is that he will work through your pain to accomplish his good purpose in your life.

God's grace to you is that he will work through your pain to accomplish his good purpose in your life.

In *Mere Christianity*, C. S. Lewis gives us this imagery:

Imagine yourself as a living house. God comes in to rebuild that house. At first, perhaps, you can understand what he is doing. He is getting the drains right and stopping the leaks in the roof and so on: you knew that those jobs needed doing and so you are not surprised. But presently he starts knocking the house about in a way that hurts abominably and does not seem to make sense. What on earth is he up to? The explanation is that he is building quite a different house from the one you thought of—throwing out a new wing here, putting on an extra floor there, running up towers, making courtyards. You thought you were going to be made into a decent little cottage, but he is building up a palace. He intends to come and live in it himself.[3]

He is at work within us to make us more like Jesus. It may not make any sense now, but just keep reading.

In some cases we'll have to keep reading all the way into eternity. The tension between "Life is hard" and "God is good" won't be fully reconciled until we are with him in heaven. But from the perspective of heaven we will finally be able to see the greatness of God's grace. Paul talks about this in 2 Corinthians 4:17–18:

> For our present troubles are small and won't last very long. Yet they produce for us a glory that vastly outweighs them and will last forever! So we don't look at the troubles we can see now; rather, we fix our gaze on things that cannot be seen. For the things we see now will soon be gone, but the things we cannot see will last forever. (NLT)

God *will* bring good out of your bad. And even if you can't currently see how God might be drawing you closer or getting glory from your pain, you still need to remember: you're in the middle. This *isn't* the end of your story. Just keep reading. Grace will have the final word.

The End of the Story

A few years ago I performed a funeral for a member of our church named Craig. He had never had any health issues, but after he experienced a few weeks of feeling fatigued and having an upset stomach, his wife urged him to visit the doctor. He went the next day and was sent to the ER for testing and a CT scan.

Within minutes he was diagnosed with stage 4 pancreatic cancer and given six months to live. He and his wife sat in a hospital room trying to process what they had just been told. With tears flowing down his cheeks, Craig told his wife that he was deciding right then to trust God no matter what the future held.

I first met Craig four months before his funeral. He and his wife introduced themselves to me after a church service. He asked if I could pray for him because he had recently been diagnosed with pancreatic cancer. Craig looked healthy and strong, and I immediately felt a connection to him. Besides being about the same age as me, Craig was a father to three beautiful girls, also just like me. I was a little more emotional than I normally would be as I prayed for God's healing.

I checked in with Craig and his wife from time to time in the months that followed. His treatment wasn't working, and he started going downhill fast. His wife was brave but scared. We talked some about how to have conversations with the three little girls about their daddy being sick. What do you say? How do you prepare them?

When I received the news of Craig's death, I was not happy with God. I'd seen him work miracles before. Why not this time?

And because I could identify with Craig, it felt more personal to me. If God's grace is greater than pancreatic cancer, why didn't God heal Craig and give him more time with his girls?

As I prepared for his funeral, I went online and read a blog Craig and his wife had started as a way to process what they were going through and communicate with others about it. After a few minutes of reading the first blog entry, I got up and shut my office door so I could cry my way through it. I was so moved by their raw honesty and especially by their faith. I eventually came to Craig's final entry.

> Just looking at myself in the mirror, I can tell my downward spiral has begun. I'm at my all time low of about 118 pounds. I have an awkward time shaving my face because it is pure bone and I feel like I'm having to shave every bony contour my face has. My yellow eyes constantly remind me my jaundice is settling back in. This pretty much means things are going to eventually start shutting down. There's nothing out there that makes sense for me to do to treat this that we haven't already looked at yet. . . .
>
> The encouragement I have that my eternal life will be in Heaven and that I will be cancer free soon puts a smile on my face. . . .
>
> I am very motivated about [w]hat the future has to offer me that there is a lot of reason to be excited.[4]

I finally arrived at the very last sentence. It was just three words followed by five exclamation points. Craig's final words:

> God is good!!!!!

Life is hard.
God is good.
Just keep reading.
Grace is greater.

NOTES

Chapter 1 More Forgiving Than Your Guilt

1. Jeremy W. Peters, "Bloomberg Plans a $50 Million Challenge to the N.R.A.," *New York Times*, April 15, 2014, http://www.nytimes.com/2014/04/16/us/bloomberg-plans-a-50-million-challenge-to-the-nra.html.

2. Saint Augustine, *Confessions*, vol. 5 (UK: Penguin, 2003), 103.

Chapter 4 More Healing Than Your Wounds

1. Jean Larroux, "Why Bad People Make Good Missionaries," sermon given at Coral Ridge Presbyterian Church, September 2014.

Chapter 5 More Freeing Than Your Bitterness

1. Natalie Angier, "If Anger Ruins Your Day, It Can Shrink Your Life," *New York Times*, December 13, 1990, http://www.nytimes.com/1990/12/13/health/if-anger-ruins-your-day-it-can-shrink-your-life.html?pagewanted=all.

2. Natalie Angier, "Chronic Anger May Lead to Early Death," *Chicago Tribune*, December 20, 1990, http://articles.chicagotribune.com/1990-12-20/news/9004150151_1_chronic-anger-early-mortality-hostile.

Chapter 6 More Prevailing Than Your Vengeance

1. Ruby Bridges, *Through My Eyes* (New York: Scholastic Press, 1999), 43.

Chapter 7   More Reconciling Than Your Resentment

1. David McCormick, "After Couple Forgave Son's Killer, All Three Were Able to Start New Life," *Los Angeles Times*, September 1, 1985, http://articles .latimes.com/1985-09-01/news/mn-25735_1_drunk-driver; see also William Plummer, "In a Supreme Act of Forgiveness, a Kentucky Couple 'Adopts' the Man Who Killed Their Son," *People*, August 26, 1985, http://www.people .com/people/archive/article/0,,20091574,00.html.

Chapter 8   More Peaceful Than Your Disappointments

1. Harvard Mental Health Letter, "In Praise of Gratitude," *Harvard Health Publications*, November 2011, http://www.health.harvard.edu/newsletter _article/in-praise-of-gratitude.

2. Ed Dobson, *Seeing through the Fog: Hope When Your World Falls Apart* (Colorado Springs: David C. Cook, 2012), 69–70.

Chapter 9   More Powerful Than Your Weakness

1. Phil Hansen, "Embrace the Shake," TED Talk, 10:01, February 2013, http://www.ted.com/talks/phil_hansen_embrace_the_shake.

2. Joni Eareckson Tada, "Joy Hard Won," *Decision*, March 2000, 12.

Chapter 10   More Hopeful Than Your Despair

1. Adoree Durayappah, "The Spoiler Paradox: How Knowing a Spoiler Makes a Story Better, Not Worse," *Huffington Post*, October 24, 2011, http:// www.huffingtonpost.com/adoree-durayappah-mapp-mba/spoiler-paradox_b _933261.html.

2. Aggie Hurst, "A Story of Eternal Perspective," Eternal Perspective Ministries, February 18, 1986, http://www.epm.org/resources/1986/Feb/18/story -eternal-perspective/. Excerpted from Aggie Hurst, *Aggie: The Inspiring Story of a Girl without a Country* (Springfield, MO: Gospel Publishing House, 1986).

3. C. S. Lewis, *Mere Christianity* (New York: Touchstone, 1996), 176.

4. Craig Merimee, "My End of the Road," *The Merimees' Journey*, February 29, 2012, http://merimeejourney.blogspot.com/2012/02/my-end-of-road.html.

Kyle Idleman is teaching pastor at Southeast Christian Church in Louisville, Kentucky, the fifth largest church in America, where he speaks to more than twenty thousand people each weekend. He is the bestselling and award-winning author of *Not a Fan* as well as *Gods at War* and *The End of Me*. He is a frequent speaker for national conventions and in influential churches across the country. Kyle and his wife, DesiRae, have four children and live on a farm in Kentucky, where he doesn't do any actual farming.

CONNECT WITH **KYLE**!

 KyleIdleman

@KyleIdleman

KyleIdleman.com

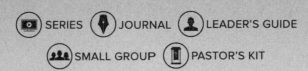